Like most Austral[...]
about Australia at [...]
versity with honou[...]
working as a politic[...]
editor of *The Sun–[...]*
announcer for ABC[...]
for *The Sydney Morning Herald*. He currently edits a daily
column called 'Stay in Touch' in *The Sydney Morning
Herald*, and contributes regularly on travel and popular
culture to the *Age* and *Who Weekly*. His nine books
include *Essential Places, An Australian in America, La
Cucina Italiana,* and *The Obsessive Traveller, or Why I
Don't Steal Towels From Great Hotels Any More.*

CATHY WILCOX was born in Sydney in 1963 and grew up
with an eye for the blank spaces between blocks of text on
a page. She has decorated spaces in at least fourteen children's books, including *A Proper Little Lady* and *Boris
and Bowch*, and provided the blocks of text as well in
Enzo The Wonderfish. Cathy now takes filling in the
blanks to its logical conclusion by drawing cartoons for
The Sydney Morning Herald (since 1989) and *The Age*
(since 1993) and has published a collection of cartoons
called *Throw Away Lines.*

THE
100
THINGS EVERYONE NEEDS TO KNOW
ABOUT
SYDNEY

DAVID DALE

Illustrations by Cathy Wilcox

PAN
Pan Macmillan Australia

First published 1997 in Pan by Pan Macmillan Australia Pty Limited
St Martins Tower, 31 Market Street, Sydney

National Library of Australia Cataloguing-in-Publication data:

Dale, David, 1948–.
    The 100 things everyone needs to know about Sydney.

    ISBN 0 330 36024 8.

    1. Sydney (N.S.W.)—Guidebooks. I. Title. II. Title: One hundred things
    everyone needs to know about Sydney.

919.4410465

Typeset in 10.2/13pt Sabon by Midland Typesetters Pty Ltd, Maryborough,
Victoria
Printed in Australia by McPherson's Printing Group

contents

CONTENTS

introduction

There are already enough guidebooks to Sydney, and by September of the year 2000 there will be three times too many. This is not one of them. I'd be delighted if this book proves useful to visitors, but I've written it primarily for Sydneysiders and for those who want to become Sydneysiders.

Guidebooks tend to get carried away about Sydney's beauty. We locals take it for granted. A fair bit of that beauty—the harbour, the beaches, the mountains, the architecture—is in these pages. But my hope is that this book will offer an insight into the *mind* of the city, rather than just its physical charms. I've looked at what Sydney eats, watches, fears, loves, gossips about, dances to and laughs at. This book is for people who want to form a relationship with Sydney, not just a one night stand.

The project grew out of an earlier book of mine, *The 100 Things Everyone Needs to Know About Australia*. While I was researching it, I kept discovering fascinating facts about the city where I have lived for more than 40 years. And I kept being surprised by how much I had forgotten or had never learned about my home town. So I set out to educate myself, and ended up with a new book that is a lot longer than the book about Australia.

I suspect most Sydneysiders are like me—happy to live where we live but rather surprised when outsiders take an interest in us. We'll be facing a rapidly rising level of outside interest over the next two years. And if we keep on taking our town for granted, we'll risk being embarrassed by our ignorance on the kind of questions our visitors will ask: 'Where did the First Fleet actually land?'; 'What's the best Italian restaurant?'; 'How do I find those designers that made Nicole Kidman's dress for the Oscars?'; 'What's that building with the temple-looking thing on its roof?'; 'Where does the Korean community live?'; 'How bad is crime here?'; 'What's this Grand Final fever all about?'; 'Who is this Fred Nile person anyway?'. I hope this book will supply the answers to most questions a visitor might ask, thereby preventing embarrassment as well as providing enlightenment.

But my view on what is essential knowledge for all Sydneysiders may be different from yours, and in every living city, things change. So *The 100 Things Everyone Needs to Know About Sydney* has to be forever a work in progress. This is the first draft, waiting to be improved by your suggestions. If you notice any gaps or errors, please write and tell me, care of the publishers. We'll get it right in the next edition or the one after.

Many other books have been helpful in my research. They include: *Book of Australian Facts*

(Reader's Digest); *The Book of Australian Firsts*, Patrick Robertson (Guinness); *The Book of Sydney Suburbs*, Frances Pollon (Angus and Robertson); *Chronicle of the 20th Century* (Penguin); *Concise History of Australia*, Russell Ward (University of Queensland Press); *The Dictionary of Australian Inventions & Discoveries*, Margaret McPhee (Allen & Unwin); *The Dictionary of Famous Australians*, Ann Atkinson (Allen & Unwin); *Eyewitness Sydney*, Ken Brass and Kirsty McKenzie (Dorling Kindersley); *The Fatal Shore*, Robert Hughes (Collins Harvill); *The Good Life Guide to Sydney*, Tessa Mountstephens (Hark! Publications); *Guide to Parks of Sydney*, Paul Knox (University of NSW Press); *New Shell Book of Firsts*, Patrick Robertson (Headline); *The SBS Eating Guide*, Maeve O'Mara and Joanna Savill (Allen & Unwin); *Seven Days in Sydney*, David Messent (self-published); *Sydney*, Jan Morris (Viking); *Sydney Architecture*, Graham Jahn (Watermark Press); *The Sydney Morning Herald Good Food Guide*, Terry Durack and Jill Dupleix (Anne O'Donovan); *Sydney Museums Guide*, Peta Landman and Michael Bogle (Kingsclear Books); *Time Out Sydney* (Penguin); *What Happened When*, Anthony Barker (Allen & Unwin).

I am particularly indebted to the Australian Bureau of Statistics, whose efforts are under-appreciated by the Australians they study. I was stimulated by these publications: *1997 NSW Year Book; Australian Demographic Trends 1997; Australian*

INTRODUCTION

Social Trends, 1997; Census of Population and Housing 1996; and *Sydney, A Social Atlas.* My special thanks go to Kirsten Tilgals, my patient and incisive editor and to Nikki Christer, dowager empress of Pan Macmillan, who agreed with my theory that Sydneysiders want to know more about their town.

DAVID DALE
AUGUST 1997

1
the name

*t*he British officers who raised a flag on 26 January 1788 on the shores of the harbour that they called Port Jackson were planning to found a city called Albion—an ancient name for England. They soon learned that the Eora people who had lived here for more than 20 000 years called the place Weerong, while the harbour was Cadi, which would make those who live around it Cadigals.

Over time all those fine names got lost. The officers named their landing spot Sydney Cove, after a second-rate bureaucrat who happened to be Britain's Home Secretary when the First Fleet set off from Plymouth in 1787. Thomas Townshend, first Baron Sydney of Chislehurst (and the last Baron Sydney too, since the title died with him) was described by his successor, Lord Grenville, as 'unequal to the most ordinary business of his office'. Somehow Sydney's name, intended only to cover the waterfront, came to cover the whole town. Albion just

1

sounded too pretentious for an open-air jail.

Dr Tim Flannery of the Australian Museum, who wrote a million-year history of Australia called *The Future Eaters*, wants the city to revert to the Aboriginal name. 'I think the name Weerong for Sydney should be put forward as a serious proposition,' Dr Flannery says. He thinks the change would symbolise that we are no longer Europeans. 'We have had to adapt to Australian conditions, we have had to become more aboriginal in the true sense of the word—a people belonging to a place'.

A change of name is not unprecedented. The place the British named Rose Hill reverted after several years to its Aboriginal name—Parramatta. I'm rather partial to the name Cadigals for we who live around the harbour. It trips off the tongue more comfortably than 'Sydneysiders'. But renaming the whole city? Are the Cadigals bold enough to take that step after more than 200 years? Perhaps Weerong sounds too much like an admission that the whole thing was a big mistake.

2
the place

S ydney is the capital of New South Wales, which is one of six states and two territories that make up the nation called Australia. One fifth of Australia's population—3.8 million people—lives here. They spread over 1740 square kilometres, bounded by the Blue Mountains to the west, the Royal National Park to the south, Broken Bay to the north and the Tasman Sea to the east.

Sydney is 16 900 km southeast of London (a 24 hour flight), 16 200 km southeast of Rome (a 23 hour flight), 12 000 km southwest of Los Angeles (a 13 hour flight), 7400 km south of Tokyo (a nine and a half hour flight), 7300 km south of Hong Kong (a nine hour flight), 1360 km west of Auckland (a three hour flight) and 870 km north of Melbourne (a one hour flight). But it contains significant contributions from all those cities.

In terms of population, it ranks 57th in the world. Tokyo is the world's biggest city, with 26.5 million people, but it takes up less space than Sydney. That's because Sydneysiders want homes with gardens—70 per cent of us live in freestanding houses, while only 20 per cent live in apartments and 10 per cent live in semidetached houses or terraces.

The suburbs have different stereotypes. The far east (around Vaucluse) is perceived to be the home of the very rich, many of European origin. The north shore includes the fairly rich, conservative voters, many of British origin. The inner eastern and inner western suburbs (where there are apartments, terraces and semis aplenty) draw the bohemians, the radicals, the academics, and the upwardly mobile. The west is home to many recent immigrants, the poor, the hardest workers. And Sydney's southern suburbs contain a mixture of the working class and the nouveau riche (and some who like to display their not-always-legal wealth by mooring boats behind their houses).

The geographical centre of Sydney is slightly west of Parramatta, but the city's heart is the harbour. At times of celebration—such as the 200th anniversary of white settlement in 1988 (when 1.5 million people gathered), the night we got the Olympics in 1993 and every New Years Eve—all corners of the city come together around the water and start to party.

BACKGROUND

3
the people

*M*ore than 140 nations have contributed to the Sydney mix, with one third of us born outside Australia and a quarter speaking a language other than English at home. Sydney's main other languages are Italian, Chinese, Arabic and Spanish. Less than one per cent of the population is Aboriginal.

About 55 000 people are born in Sydney every year (20 per cent of them to couples who are not married), and 26 000 people die (mostly of cancer and heart disease). Half of our 3.8 million residents are under 34, making Sydney a younger city than Adelaide but older than Canberra. Some 12 per cent of the population is over 65, and they tend to live in northern suburbs such as Manly, Lindfield and Hunters Hill and southern suburbs such as Kogarah and Sans Souci. Seven per cent is under four years of age, and they tend to live in the outer western areas. In fact, Australia's biggest breeders live in Liverpool and Blacktown, suburbs

5

which have the nation's highest rate of growth in the infant age bracket.

Ten per cent of Sydney homes contain people who are living alone. Another 10 per cent are one-parent families (tending to live around Blacktown and Campbelltown in the outer west, and Redfern and Waterloo in the inner suburbs).

About 42 per cent of households contain couples with children, and eight per cent are DINKs (double income, no kids) who can afford to live in the inner eastern suburbs of Potts Point and Paddington, the lower north shore, and the inner western suburbs of Annandale, Balmain and Newtown.

About 250 000 people in Sydney—15 per cent of the population—have university degrees, and they tend to live in northern suburbs such as Chatswood, Pymble and Wahroonga, or inner suburbs such as Glebe, Balmain and Bellevue Hill.

And how do all these people spend their money? The Australian Bureau of Statistics surveyed Sydneysiders in the mid 1990s and found the average household spent $669 a week, of which 3 per cent went on alcohol, 6 per cent on clothing, 13 per cent on recreation and 15 per cent on transport. We spent more on housing (17 per cent of the weekly budget) and food and drink (19 per cent) than any other state capital. It's expensive to live in Australia's most interesting city.

4
the originals

*t*he area that came to be known as Sydney had been settled for more than 20 000 years before Europeans arrived. Around the harbour lived the Eora people, to the north lived the Daruk, and to the south lived the Tharawal—a total population of about 3000. They used caves for shelter rather than building permanent structures, and lived by collecting local plants and shellfish, or by fishing from flat canoes that looked a lot like modern surfboards. Their diet was more varied and nutritious than that of most Europeans, and their lifestyle gave them plenty of exercise, so these indigenous people tended to be taller and healthier than the new arrivals. They greeted the British with mild curiosity in the main, and there were few incidents of violence. Governor Phillip, under orders from London to 'conciliate their affections, enjoining all our subjects to live in amity and kindness with them', severely punished any convicts who maltreated the locals. But by 1789, black corpses were a common sight around the settlement, as the Aboriginal people fell victim to smallpox, cholera and influenza.

The first serious resistance seems to have been organised by an Eora leader named Pemulwuy in

1790. He led guerilla attacks on white settlers and property until his capture and beheading in 1802. That resistance struggle was dealt a final blow with the capture of his son Tedbury in 1805.

There are now no known descendants of the Eora in Sydney. Although more Aboriginal people live here than in any other Australian city, the population of about 34 000 is descended from displaced inland communities who headed for the big towns throughout the 1900s. The word *koori* or *koorie* is now often used to describe the Aboriginal peoples of some parts of Victoria and New South Wales, including Sydney, although this is not universally accepted, even within the Aboriginal community.

Most of Sydney's Aboriginal population lives around Redfern and the outer western suburbs. Their profile has risen since the 1980s through increased media attention on Aboriginal political activism, dance, art and music ('from rock artists to rock artists').

The media have also focused on the area around Eveleigh Street, Redfern, calling it 'the South Bronx of Australia'. Unemployment is high here, and so is alcoholism and drug dealing. The whites whose handbags are snatched or whose cars are robbed as they pass through may gain a small impression of the high rate of crime, the major victims of which are Aboriginal families.

5

a start

e uropean settlement in Sydney began with a real estate con and a wild party—two themes that became quite familiar in the city's life over the ensuing two centuries.

When Captain Arthur Phillip led his fleet into Botany Bay on Friday 18 January 1788, he was expecting to find a magnificent harbour surrounded by fertile plains and rolling hills. This was the bay where James Cook and Joseph Banks—often cited as the European discoverers of Eastern Australia—had first landed in 1770. They had written about a protected anchorage, an ample source of building stone, and grassland with deep black soil and well-spaced trees, where crops could be planted without clearing. Instead Phillip found a shallow inlet surrounded by swampy windswept sandhills. And it was already occupied. Phillip remarked that 'the natives are far more numerous than they were supposed to be'. These particular locals didn't even speak the language Cook had recorded. Their name for the animal Cook claimed they called a *kangaroo* was *patagarang*. Some of them yelled *warra, warra* at the crew of the flagship *Sirius*—a phrase which the British later decided meant 'go away' when it was accompanied by spear hurling.

Phillip knew he had to find another site fast and set off northwards in a small boat to explore Port Jackson, a bay which had been named but not investigated by Cook and which we now think of as Sydney Harbour. After landing at Camp Cove, just inside what is now South Head, Phillip was pretty impressed and decided to shift the colony there. The fleet sailed around, and the British Union flag was raised near what is now the Customs House at Circular Quay on the afternoon of Saturday, 26 January.

The women and children stayed on the ships for another two weeks until tents and huts had been erected for them. Late on Wednesday, 6 February, they finally came ashore. It was a dark and stormy night, but the weather did not deter the immigrants from celebrating the women's landfall. With an extra issue of rum for the sailors, it was party time. 'It is beyond my abilities to give a just description of the scene of debauchery and riot that ensued during the night,' wrote the surgeon, Arthur Bowes Smyth.

Next morning, the convicts got a lecture from the governor. There would be no repetition of the previous night's activities, and any prisoner who tried to enter the women's tents would be shot. Then Phillip and his officers, sweating in full uniform, sat down to a lunch of roast mutton, from sheep which had been killed the day before. The meat was already crawling with maggots. The British were beginning to get the impression they weren't meant to be here.

6

the convicts

*t*he British Cabinet voted in August 1786 to set up a penal colony in New South Wales to serve as 'a remedy for the evils likely to result from the late alarming and numerous increase of felons in this country, and more particularly in the metropolis'. And so began an 80-year program to relieve the pressure on Britain's prisons after America ceased to be available as a dumping ground for society's nuisances.

The first instalment left Portsmouth on 13 May 1787—11 ships under the command of Captain Arthur Phillip. They carried 20 members of Phillip's staff, 210 crew members, 233 merchant seamen, 206 soldiers (with 27 wives and 19 children), 770 convicts (191 of them women) and 13 children of the convicts. During the journey, 23 convicts and two of their children died, while six children were born. All the ships reached Botany Bay by 20 January 1788.

The Second Fleet, which arrived in June 1790, didn't fare so well. Of the 1006 prisoners who sailed from Portsmouth, 267 died at sea and another 150 died soon after landing in a colony which was desperately short of food and medicine.

How bad were the criminals that Britain

dumped? They had all been convicted of more than one crime, and many habitual offenders had originally been sentenced to death, which was commuted to transportation. Yet none of the First Fleeters had committed rape or murder.

The most frequent offences were theft, breaking and entering, and highway robbery. One 70-year-old woman got seven years exile for stealing 12 pounds of cheese, one man got the same for stealing two hens. None of the women were prostitutes, although some may have taken up the trade after they arrived.

There were no political prisoners in the early days, but after 1795, the British Government started taking the opportunity to get rid of English trade unionists and Irish rebels. A total of 30 000 men and 9000 women were transported to Australia from Ireland, most of them petty thieves but about 20 per cent social dissidents. Those 8000 Irish revolutionaries played a big role in the new nation's political consciousness.

In 1804, a group of 260 Irish convicts started a rebellion at Parramatta aimed at overthrowing the governor, but they were quickly defeated by the NSW Corps under Major George Johnston (who, ironically, led a military coup against Governor Bligh four years later). Most of those involved in Australia's first and only convict uprising were hanged, but, as Robert Hughes points out in *The Fatal Shore*, 'the sense of a community divided between English Protestant "haves" and Irish Catholic "have-nots" began with them and influenced the patterns of power in Australian life for another 150 years'.

The convicts either worked for the government or were assigned as slaves to free settlers, mostly on building or farming projects. If they behaved well, they could receive a ticket of leave, a kind of probation which meant they could work for wages. Finally they could be granted a conditional pardon, which meant they could do anything they liked except return to England. A small number earned full pardons. Those who failed to conform were executed or sent to the worse concentration camps at Norfolk Island and Van Diemen's Land (Tasmania).

By the time transportation to NSW officially ended in 1840 (it continued in other states until 1868), some 83 000 convicts had been sent here, while only 70 000 settlers had arrived of their own free will. So it is true to say that until well into the 20th century, the majority of Sydneysiders were descended from small-time criminals.

7

200 years in 600 words

*i*t almost went nowhere. When Governor Arthur Phillip, sick and tired, left Sydney Cove in 1792, there was little reason to think that this concentration camp in the south seas could survive without constant infusions from Britain. A few struggling farms at Parramatta could not meet the colony's food needs. There was nothing to justify the optimism of the first free settlers who arrived in January 1793—five men, one woman and two children from England who were given a land grant in what is now called Strathfield but was then called Liberty Plains.

In 1795, Sydney produced its first export—a shipment of mahogany and cedar from trees cut along the Hawkesbury River, sent off to make British boats and furniture. It was soon followed by shipments of whale and seal products, which formed the basis of the Sydney economy for the first 30 years.

What changed things was the merino. The sheep carried to Sydney by the first few fleets were simply for eating, but John Macarthur and Samuel Marsden bought a small flock of merinos from the Cape of Good Hope in 1798 and started breeding.

The first commercial shipment of wool left in 1807, and within 40 years, Sydney was supplying half of the wool used in the clothing mills of Britain. By the early 20th century, wool was providing 60 per cent of Australia's export income.

In 1803, Australia's first newspaper, *The Sydney Gazette and NSW Advertiser*, was published, but the first convincing evidence that Sydney had a future came with the establishment of the Bank of NSW in 1817, followed by Campbells Bank (the forerunner of the present State Bank) in 1819. By the 1830s, there was a growing sense in Europe that Sydney might be a place where you could get rich quick. In 1842 (two years after the convicts stopped arriving) Sydney was officially incorporated as a city, and a year later, the first elected Legislative Council began to take over the powers of the governor.

The 1850s saw a gold rush just west of the Blue Mountains, and when that petered out, coal mining became a useful source of income, helped by the spread of the railways in the 1860s. Between 1860 and 1890, Sydney's popu-lation rose from 100 000 to 400 000, inspiring a build-ing boom which hardly faltered during the depres-sion of the 1890s. In 1901, Sydney was the scene of the official celebrations for the federation of six

colonies into a new nation called Australia.

The new national government (temporarily operating from Melbourne) decided to base the Commonwealth Bank in Sydney in 1912, and by the 1920s, we were Australia's richest and most hedonistic town. In 1922, the visiting British author D H Lawrence wrote that 'Sydney goes by itself, loose and easy, without any bossing'.

Sydney scraped through the Great Depression more comfortably than other Australian cities due to the jobs created by the construction of the Harbour Bridge and the underground railway system. And once the Bridge was opened in 1932, the north of the Harbour could be developed.

But for all its wealth and energy, the city lacked diversity. The vast majority of its citizens were of English or Irish background, which meant a blandness in the cooking, the culture, and the range of ideas. This began to change in 1947 when the national government, under the slogan 'populate or perish', encouraged massive immigration from Europe. Over 30 years, a million new arrivals—many of them speaking Italian, Greek or a Yugoslav language—transformed the city. And when the immigration program expanded in the 1970s to include the Middle East and Asia, Sydney could look forward to becoming a city of infinite surprises.

8

the names to know—dead

*W*e don't know the names of the key figures in the Sydney area during the first 20 000 years of human habitation, but in the first 100 years of European settlement, these people made a difference:

☆ **ARTHUR PHILLIP,** the first ruler. Born in 1738, he learned sailing at the Establishment for Poor Boys in Greenwich, near London, and served in the British and Portuguese navies. He became a surveyor in the Admiralty in 1786 and was appointed to run the prison camp at Botany Bay. Phillip captained the first fleet of convict ships, decided to camp in Port Jackson instead of Botany Bay, and became the colony's first governor, but retired through ill health in 1792. The air back in London did wonders for him, because he rejoined the British navy and reached the rank of Rear Admiral by 1801. There is a statue of him in our Botanic Gardens.

☆ **LE COMTE DE LA PEROUSE,** the man who nearly changed everything. Two days after

Arthur Phillip's fleet reached Botany Bay, the British were amazed to see two French ships, *La Boussole* and *L'Astrolabe*, sailing towards the shore. They were under the command of Jean-François de Galaup, the Count of La Perouse, who was exploring for France. Sydneysiders enjoy speculating how different the city would have been if the French had got here a few days earlier. La Perouse and his shipmates stayed six weeks, then sailed off and got killed in a shipwreck near what is now Vanuatu. La Perouse got a bleak suburb named after him, and the French erected a large monument to him there in 1825.

☆ **BENNELONG,** the first ambassador between the locals and the invaders. A member of the Eora people in his mid twenties, he was captured at Manly in November 1789 and taken to live with Governor Phillip, who built him a house on what is now the site of the Opera House. Bennelong rapidly learned English and acted as a guide on local customs. Phillip took him and another Eora man, Yemerrawanie, to London in 1792, where they met King George III. Bennelong returned to Sydney in 1795 with Governor Hunter and wrote in a letter to the steward of Lord Sydney in London: 'I have not my wife. Another black man took her away. We have muzzy doings; he speared me in the back, but I better now. All my friends alive and well. Not me go to England no more. I am home now'. He had trouble adjusting to a split existence between white and black cultures and died in 1813, apparently an alcoholic.

☆ **JAMES RUSE**, the first farmer. Convicted of breaking and entering, he was transported with the First Fleet. Phillip gave him a farm at Parramatta as an experiment to see how long it would take to become self sufficient. Ruse grew Australia's first successful wheat crop in 1790, then got a land grant which he ultimately lost through business incompetence.

☆ **WILLIAM BLIGH**, the despot. Because he'd sailed round the world with James Cook in 1773, and because he'd survived the mutiny on the *Bounty* in 1789, the British Government thought Bligh would be tough enough to bring the colony's corrupt military unit, the NSW Corps, under control. Bligh became governor in 1805 at the age of 52, but failed to break the power of the Corps (which controlled the rum trade) and was overthrown in the Rum Rebellion of 1808. He returned to England, gave evidence against the rebel leaders, and got promoted to Admiral.

☆ **JOHN MACARTHUR**, the first entrepreneur,

whose wealth, ambition and influence over government is echoed by some of Sydney's modern moguls. Macarthur arrived in 1790 as an officer in the NSW Corps, bred the first merinos that started Sydney's wool industry, organised the military coup that overthrew Governor Bligh, and was forcibly returned to England between 1809 and 1817 (while his wife Elizabeth ran the Sydney business). After his return, he became a member of the Legislative Council that advised the governor but was dismissed in 1832 after being 'pronounced a lunatic'. The Macarthurs' first farmhouse is preserved at Parramatta. It is named after Elizabeth because she did most of the work there while John was arguing with the authorities.

☆ **MARY REIBEY**, the first businesswoman. Mary Haydock was sentenced to seven years transportation for stealing a horse, and reached Sydney in 1792 at the age of 15. She soon married a free settler named Thomas Reibey, who died in 1811, leaving her with seven children and a wine and spirits business in The Rocks. She expanded it into an empire, becoming a shipowner, property developer, merchant and landlord. It was in one of Reibey's buildings that the Bank of NSW started in 1817.

☆ **LACHLAN MACQUARIE**, the visionary

builder. Macquarie arrived as governor in 1810 with his own regiment, which enabled him to bring the NSW Corps under control. He started an elaborate program of town planning and construction, recognising his own contribution by naming landmarks after himself or his wife Elizabeth. But he clashed with John Macarthur, who thought convicts should be working for private citizens and not on government projects, and was accused of extravagance by a commission of inquiry in 1820, which forced his resignation. There's a statue of him in Macquarie Street, near Hunter Street.

☆ **WILLIAM CHARLES WENTWORTH**, the first politician. In 1813, at the age of 20, he became a local hero by leading an expedition across the Blue Mountains and was rewarded with a large land grant. In 1824, he started the colony's first independent newspaper, *The Australian*, and campaigned for trial by jury (which was granted in 1830) and representative government (a form of which was granted in 1842). In 1843, he was elected to the Legislative Council and helped draft the NSW constitution which created the first parliament in 1855, although his proposal for a colonial peerage system, nicknamed 'the bunyip aristocracy', was rejected. His home, Vaucluse House, is now a national monument.

☆ **HENRY PARKES,** the nation maker. He emigrated to Australia from Britain in 1839, aged 24, and was running an ivory-turning shop in Sydney in 1854 when he was elected to NSW parliament on a ticket of radical reform. He was appointed Colonial Secretary in 1866 and ended state aid to religious schools. As Premier of NSW, on and off between 1872 and 1889, Parkes campaigned for the unification of the colonies into 'a great national government for all Australia', but died in 1896, four years before his scheme was implemented. There's a statue of him in Centennial Park.

9
the topic

*W*hat Sydney people talk about most at barbecues and dinner parties is house prices. This city has one of the highest rates of ownership (or almost-ownership) in the world—38 per cent of homes are wholly owned, 25 per cent are being paid off, and 28 per cent are being rented. So almost everyone has a reason to discuss property. The owners are wondering if it's the right time to sell, the recent buyers are comparing renovations, the mortgage-payers are wondering if their interest rates are too high, and the renters are spending their Saturday mornings visiting houses they may never afford.

Here's some basic data to help you enter the typical Sydney conversation. The median price of a home here is $260 000—the highest of any Australian city. A 1997 study by Sydney University's Planning Research Centre showed that a couple would need an annual income of more than $45 000 before they could even think about buying a

home anywhere in Sydney. To be able to rent a one-bedroom house in the inner suburbs, they'd need $35 000 a year, while $25 000 would limit them to renting a one-bedroom apartment on the city's fringe.

As of 1997, the fashionable spots to seek house bargains were inner western suburbs such as Marrickville and Dulwich Hill. Between 1978 and 1996, house prices rose 30 per cent on the lower north shore, 7 per cent on the upper north shore, 27 per cent in central Sydney, 38 per cent in the eastern suburbs, 33 per cent in the inner west, 11 per cent in the Parramatta area, and 16 per cent in the south around Cronulla. But in the northwestern Hills district, prices declined 2 per cent.

Once the subject of property prices has been debated to exhaustion, Sydney people can move on to their second favourite conversational activity: badmouthing the rich and famous.

10
the goss

Sydney might just be the urban myth capital of the world. But we specialise in a particular kind of mythology. This big tough city, which is so cynical about most things, throws away its scepticism when it hears tales about the hypocrisy or the perversity of the rich, the powerful and the famous.

We love to talk about the prominent businessman who strangled his girlfriend's cat to punish her for rejecting him; and the television host who liked to lie under a glass-topped coffee table while women stood on it and urinated; and the state premier who received $5000 in a brown paper bag every week in return for keeping the police away from the illegal gambling casinos; and the former Liberal Party leader who liked rough sex and who broke a prostitute's jaw in a room in the poshest hotel in town.

When we hear stories like that, we ignore common sense and spread them assiduously and uncritically to our friends and acquaintances. In the 1980s, several journalists spent a fair amount of time trying to check out a rumour that Paul Landa, the then Attorney-General of NSW, had died on the tennis court of Abe Saffron, a man described as a major criminal in several public inquiries. Now Paul

Landa did in fact die of a heart attack on a tennis court, and there were allegations that Landa was corrupt, both as Attorney-General and in his former role as Planning and Environment Minister. But whatever people may have accused him of, nobody ever accused Landa of being a complete idiot, and the notion that an attorney-general would risk being seen playing tennis with the man known as 'Mr Sin' is just absurd. Still, Sydney took it seriously.

In the month of February 1997, in my capacity as a columnist for *The Sydney Morning Herald*, I heard the following rumours: a former political leader (male) was regularly seen holding hands with a young man in various Sydney restaurants; the father-in-law of another political leader had threatened to stop raising funds for the party unless the politician stopped having an affair with his secretary; another former political leader had turned gay and had an affair with a pianist or alternatively a violinist from the Sydney Symphony Orchestra; a former political leader had left his wife because *she* had an affair with a pianist or a violinist; a former political leader was having an affair with a TV newsreader (then the person who told me that rumour phoned to correct it—actually the politician was having an affair with a magazine editor whose name sounded similar to that of the newsreader); a former political leader was having an affair with a prominent businesswoman; a former political leader was being treated for clinical depression. And, in a twist that I particularly liked, a rumour that all those rumours about the former political leader's affairs were being spread by the wife of another former political leader.

These are the campfire fables that bind the Sydney tribe together. We can trace this style of storytelling back to the convict days, when the only way the inmates of the prison camp could fight back against their jailers was to spread malicious stories about them. We all know what's going on between Governor Phillip and Bennelong, don't we? You know why Governor Macquarie keeps having those fits of rage, don't you? He's in the tertiary stages of syphilis. Everybody knows why these dreadful buildings are going up around the harbour—Francis Greenway is in the pocket of the developers. What do you think John Macarthur is doing out there at Parramatta with all those sheep he's importing? Or is he just spinning a yarn?

Another name for this sort of behaviour is the tall poppy syndrome, which I think is Australia's health-iest national trait. Aust-ralians don't make heroes easily. Being sceptical about our prominent figures is a great protection against the disappointment that Ameri-cans so often feel when the people they worship turn out to have scandalous private

More Australian Urban Mythology

A magpie took my baby

27

lives. When you start, as Sydneysiders do, from the assumption that everyone is corrupt or perverse, you can only be pleasantly surprised.

I think we often repeat these rumours as one might tell a fairytale to a child—to entertain and to convey a moral message. Every time we recount these fables, we are celebrating a 200-year-old folk tradition. In Australia, spreading scandals has the same heritage significance as clog dancing in Holland, or changing the guard at Buckingham Palace, or drinking beer in Munich during Oktoberfest. We may laugh or cringe, but if we stop doing it, we lose a precious symbol of our national identity.

I think it's time we turned this Sydney tradition into a money-maker. We should set up an annual festival of malicious gossip. It could be called Skandalfest. The posters advertising it would be decorated with a tall poppy and an approaching axe to cut it down to size. Tourists from every nation would flock to see it. All defamation laws would be suspended for that week, and the rich and the powerful would be expected to take whatever was thrown at them, for the sake of the economy.

Perhaps rumour-mongering should be made an event for the year 2000 Olympics. The local team would certainly win the gold medal.

11
the names to know—alive

*l*ater chapters in this book deal with Sydney's stars and Sydney's heroes. This one covers people who just can't seem to stay out of the media.

☆ **THE WHITLAMS**, Australia's elder statesfolk. Gough Whitlam was Labor prime minister between 1972 and 1975, recognised as a visionary social reformer with a blind spot for economics. His wife Margaret has contributed her wisdom to a variety of charitable causes. He launches books and gives keynote addresses. They are easily identified at premieres because they are taller than everyone else.

☆ **GAI WATERHOUSE**, Sydney's most visible racehorse trainer. The successful daughter of the legendary trainer Tommy Smith and the wife of a bookmaker who was barred from racetracks for allegedly trying to fix a race (known as the Fine Cotton Affair), she wears big hats to racing carnivals.

☆ **MALCOLM TURNBULL**, an aggressive lawyer and merchant banker, formerly a business associate of Kerry Packer. He now

leads the campaign to make Australia a
republic.

☆ **JOHN SINGLETON**, who runs an advertising
agency and two Sydney radio stations, 2CH
and 2GB. He's famed for using the 'ocker'
image to sell products, and for his love of fast
cars.

☆ **LEO SCHOFIELD**, Sydney's top networker. A
former advertising copywriter, public relations
exec and restaurant critic, he moved briefly to
Melbourne in the early 1990s to run arts
festivals but was then made boss of the Sydney
Festival from 1998 and of the cultural events
around the Olympic Games in 2000. He has a
knack of befriending junior politicians on their
way up.

☆ **FRANK SARTOR**, Lord Mayor of Sydney,
although Sydney, in this case, means the central
business district, which contains about 4000
voters. Sartor has turned a minor job into a
major public profile.

☆ **IAN ROBERTS**, described by the media as
'Australia's first openly gay footballer'. He's a
big bruiser who has played rugby league for
South Sydney, Manly Warringah and
Australia's international Test team. His decision
to discuss his 'inner city lifestyle' in a 1997
book called *Ian Roberts: Finding Out*, was
risky because league fans tend to be socially
conservative. But it has gained him work as a

photographic model. And if anyone objects to his sexual preference, they can just try telling him to his face.

☆ **SUSAN RENOUF**, a socialite sometimes referred to as Lady Renouf, as if part of some aristocracy. She has been married to a Liberal politician (Andrew Peacock), an English horseracing figure (Robert Sangster) and a New Zealand businessman (Sir Frank Renouf) with whom she squabbled publicly in 1987 over possession of his Sydney mansion, 'Paradis Sur Mer'.

☆ **NEIL PERRY**, the definitive restaurateur. The model of the modern Sydney chef is a pony-tailed youth who charms the media as cleverly as he chargrills an octopus. Neil Perry created that model. His first triumph was Rockpool, an expensive seafood restaurant that won all the gourmet awards. Then he created an empire, with the cafe at the Museum of Contemporary Art, and Wockpool, the trendy Asian bistro at Darling Harbour.

☆ **FRED AND ELAINE NILE**, Sydney's most public puritans, and campaigners against pornography, abortion and homosexuality. Fred and then Elaine (who follows her husband in everything) were elected to the upper house of the NSW parliament as representatives of a party called Call To Australia, an offshoot of Fred's Christian lobby group, the Festival of Light.

☆ **LACHLAN MURDOCH,** the son of Rupert Murdoch and boss of News Limited's Australian operations.

☆ **CLOVER MOORE,** the stirrer. She is the independent member of parliament for the inner city electorate of Bligh, so she has become a voice for the gays and bohemians who live there. And her voice is influential. Owing nothing to any power groupings, she was able to speak against Rupert Murdoch's plans to build a film studio in the area near Centennial Park that was formerly the Royal Agricultural Society's Show Ground, where the Easter Show was held until 1997.

☆ **HARRY M MILLER,** an entertainment entrepreneur who staged the first production of *Hair* in Sydney in 1969. In 1982, he was found guilty of misappropriation of funds connected with his failed ticket agency Computicket and jailed for 10 months. He now acts as agent for people seeking to be paid for media appearances.

☆ **MAX MARKSON,** who runs a public relations firm and acts as agent for would-be celebrities. He is sometimes known as the poor man's Harry M Miller.

☆ **SONIA McMAHON,** a socialite, the widow of

the former Liberal Prime Minister William McMahon, and mother of the soap opera actor Julian McMahon.

☆ **ROD McGEOCH**, a tall lawyer who was one of the organisers of Sydney's successful bid for the year 2000 Olympics. He now heads a business lobby group called the Sydney Committee.

☆ **LEONIE KRAMER**, the conservative academic. Former Professor of Australian Literature at the University of Sydney and now its chancellor, she can be relied on to support traditional values when appointed by Liberal governments to boards and committees.

☆ **KIM HOLLINGSWORTH**, who was training to become a NSW police officer but was dismissed because the police authorities were shocked to discover she used to be a prostitute and striptease dancer. The NSW Industrial Commission ruled in 1997 that her sacking was 'unfair, harsh, unreasonable or unjust' because she had been working as an undercover agent and had exposed connections between several police officers and the vice industry.

☆ **KATHRYN GREINER**, who leads the conservative group on the Sydney City Council and could be Lord Mayor one day. She is married to **Nick Greiner,** who was forced to resign as Liberal Premier of NSW after he was accused of offering a public service job to an independent politician to increase his support in parliament. He is now chairman of the tobacco company W D & H O Wills. The Greiners publicly separated in 1995 when Nick became involved with a younger woman, but they publicly reunited late in 1996.

☆ **GLEN-MARIE FROST**, famous in the 1970s as the mistress of Ian Sinclair (the leader of the National Party) and in the 1980s as a PR lady who lunched in the smartest places. She is now the public relations director for the Sydney Organising Committee for the Olympic Games.

☆ **KATE FISCHER**, the city's top party girl of the 1990s. A model who appeared topless in the film *Sirens*, Fischer was originally best known for displaying her cleavage in magazine photos, but became even better known for becoming engaged to **James Packer**, the son of Australia's richest man (Kerry Packer) and the managing director of PBL, the Packer media empire.

☆ **EDMUND CAPON**, the expert. As director of the Art Gallery of NSW, he has to be visible at opening nights and offer urbane commentary on artistic fads and pretensions.

☆ **ITA BUTTROSE**, a grand lady, famous for being 'former'. She is the former editor of *Cleo* magazine, the *Women's Weekly*, the *Sunday Telegraph*, the *Sun Herald* and *Ita* magazine, and the former chair of the National Advisory Committee on AIDs. In the mid 1990s she was doing TV advertisements for cosmetics.

12
scandals

*h*ere's a selection of the human dramas which have preoccupied Sydney over recent decades.

☆ **THE THALLIUM FAD.** A passion for a poison called thallium seemed to break out among Sydney women in the 1950s. Yvonne Fletcher, 32, was charged in June 1952 with murdering her first husband, Desmond, and her second husband Bert. Her defence was curious: that Bert must have found out that thallium killed Desmond and used it to kill himself in order to incriminate Yvonne. She was sentenced to death. Then in July 1953, Caroline Grills, 63, was charged with killing her sister-in-law and three others with thallium. Police alleged she did it because she enjoyed watching the poison's effect on her victims. 'Aunt Thally', as she was tagged, was also sentenced to death.

☆ **THE THORNE KIDNAPPING.** In July 1960, an 11-year-old boy called Graeme Thorne, son of a couple who had won 100 000 pounds in the lottery, was kidnapped by someone who demanded 25 000 pounds ransom. The boy's body was found in a cave a month later, after he had apparently suffocated in the boot of a car. A man named Stephen Bradley was arrested in Colombo and ultimately sentenced to life imprisonment.

☆ **THE OZ TRIAL.** In 1964, the three young editors of the satirical *OZ* magazine—Richard Neville, Richard Walsh and Martin Sharp— were sentenced to jail terms of up to six months for producing an obscene publication. The sentences were overturned on appeal. Neville went on to a similar experience with a London edition of *OZ*, Walsh became the publisher of Kerry Packer's magazines, and Sharp became a successful artist.

☆ **THE ASSASSINATION ATTEMPT.** In 1966, a youth named Peter Kocan tried to shoot the Labor Party leader Arthur Calwell as he was leaving an anti-conscription rally at Mosman Town Hall. Kocan was released years later after psychiatric treatment and wrote stories which became high school texts.

☆ **THE WOOLWORTH'S EXTORTION.** During 1980, bombs went off in three Woolworth's department stores and the company was told this would keep happening if they did not pay $1 million. In 1981, police arrested Gregory McHardy and Larry Danielsen as they were trying to collect the ransom money at Taronga Zoo Wharf. They were sentenced to 20 years jail.

✫ **THE WRAN INQUIRY**. In 1983, the Labor leader Neville Wran stepped down as Premier of NSW and submitted himself to a royal commission after the ABC television program *Four Corners* alleged that the Chief Magistrate of Sydney had used Wran's name in an attempt to influence the trial of a rugby league official. The Royal Commission found no evidence against Wran (earning him the nickname 'Never Rang'). The Chief Magistrate, Murray Farquhar, was sentenced to four years jail for trying to pervert the course of justice.

✫ **THE EARLY RELEASE SCHEME**. In 1984, the Minister for Corrective Services, Rex Jackson, was accused of receiving bribes to release certain prisoners early, and in 1987 he was sentenced to ten years jail.

✫ **THE ANITA COBBY KILLING**. In 1986, five men—John Travers, Michael Murdoch and the brothers Leslie, Gary and Michael Murphy— were sentenced to life imprisonment for the rape and murder of a nurse named Anita Cobby at Prospect in the outer western suburbs.

✫ **DEEP SLEEP THERAPY**. A royal commission in 1990 condemned the health authorities for failing to stop doctors at Chelmsford private hospital using a therapy method for chronic depression which involved putting patients into drug-induced comas. Of 1127 patients who received the treatment over 16 years, 26 died.

Dr Harry Bailey, who had pioneered the therapy, committed suicide in 1985.

☆ **THE FALL OF McBRIDE.** Dr William McBride, who became an international hero in 1961 for finding the connection between the drug Thalidomide and birth deformities, was struck off the medical register in 1990 over allegations of fraud in his research into Debendox, another anti-nausea drug used during pregnancy.

☆ **THE GRANNY KILLER.** In 1990, John Wayne Glover was sentenced to life imprisonment for stalking and murdering six elderly ladies in the Mosman area.

☆ **THE METHERELL AFFAIR.** In 1992, the Liberal Party leader Nick Greiner was forced to resign as Premier of NSW after the Independent Commission Against Corruption found that he had offered a public service job to Terry Metherell, an independent MP, in order to get Metherell out of parliament and replace him with a Liberal member. The Supreme Court later found that Greiner had not acted corruptly.

☆ **THE YELDHAM SUICIDE.** In November 1996, a judge named David Yeldham committed suicide after the Royal Commission into the NSW Police Service began investigating whether police had covered up incidents where Yeldham had propositioned men in public toilets.

13
mysteries

*t*his is your town if you like the challenge of pondering crimes that stay unsolved for years—and not always because someone paid the police to leave them that way. Here's a sampling:

☆ **THE BOGLE-CHANDLER DEATHS.** Early on 1 January 1963, two bodies were found in bush on the Lane Cove River, near Chatswood Golf Course. The man was wearing only underpants, socks and shoes, the woman had her dress rolled up to the waist. They were Gilbert Bogle, a CSIRO scientist, and Margaret Chandler, the wife of another CSIRO scientist. They had known each other only three weeks, so a suicide pact seems unlikely. Poisoned, presumably (both had vomited shortly before their deaths). But with what, and why? Were they military researchers, killed to protect a secret? Not even the recent opening of the files of the KGB has provided a clue.

☆ **THE WANDA BEACH MURDERS.** On 12 January 1965, the raped and slashed bodies of two fifteen-year-olds, Marianne Schmidt and Christine Sharrock, were found in sand dunes behind Wanda Beach, near Cronulla.

☆ **THE DISAPPEARANCE OF JUANITA NIELSEN.** Nielsen was editor of an inner city newspaper called *Now* which campaigned against property developments that would have destroyed historic homes in the Kings Cross area. On 4 July 1975, she disappeared. One theory is that she is buried under the foundations of one of the high rises she opposed.

☆ **THE HILTON BOMBING.** On 13 July 1978, a bomb exploded in a garbage can outside the Hilton Hotel in Sydney, where a Commonwealth Heads of Government meeting was being held. Two garbage collectors and a police officer were killed. A former member of the Ananda Marga sect was later convicted of the bombing (it was supposedly aimed at the Prime Minister of India) but suspicions remain of involvement by Australia's secret service agencies.

☆ **THE ATTACKS ON THE FAMILY COURT.** On 23 June 1980, Judge David Opas of the Family Court opened his front door in Woollahra and was shot dead. Then in March 1984, Judge Richard Gee of the same court was injured in a bomb blast that wrecked his Belrose home. In April 1984, the Family Court building in Parramatta was damaged by a bomb; and in July, Pearl Watson, wife of the Family Court Judge Ray Watson, was killed when a bomb exploded outside their Greenwich home. It would seem that someone is not happy with their divorce property settlement.

☆ **THE DEATH OF BILLY SNEDDEN.** On 27 June 1987, the body of Snedden, a former leader of the Liberal Party and Speaker of Federal Parliament, was found in a motel room at Rushcutters Bay. He was wearing only a condom and had apparently died of a heart attack. He had checked into the motel with a woman who has never identified herself.

☆ **THE SHOOTING OF JOHN NEWMAN.** Newman was the State Labor Party MP for Cabramatta. In September 1994, he was campaigning for greater police action against Vietnamese drug dealers in his area when he was shot dead outside his house by a group of men in a passing car. His fiancee, Lucy Wang, saw the shooting from a distance, but wasn't wearing her glasses at the time.

☆ **AND ONE FOR THE X-FILES.** On 30 August 1955, an Auster aircraft took off from Bankstown airport without pilot or passengers. It flew over Sydney for three hours before being shot down by a navy jet.

14
disasters

*t*errible things happen on a large scale in the history of any big city. Sometimes they are nobody's fault, though some of these examples had a human cause.

☆ **THE SINKING OF THE GREYCLIFFE**. On 3 November 1927, a wooden ferry named *Greycliffe*, carrying 150 passengers from Circular Quay to Watson's Bay, was rammed by the steamer *Tahiti*, heading out of the harbour for San Francisco. The ferry sank in 30 seconds and 37 people drowned.

☆ **THE MIDGET SUBS**. On 31 May 1942, three Japanese midget submarines entered Sydney Harbour. One of them fired a torpedo at an American warship moored in the harbour but missed and hit a ferry called *Kuttabul*, which sank, killing 19 Australian naval officers. Two of the subs were blown up and the third escaped.

☆ **THE GRANVILLE TRAIN SMASH**. Early on 18 January 1977, a train heading for Sydney from the Blue Mountains left the line and rammed a pylon supporting an overpass near Granville railway station. The driver was unharmed but the road collapsed onto the third and fourth carriages, killing 83 people.

☆ **THE LUNA PARK FIRE**. On 9 June 1979, a father, his two sons and four friends died when a fire broke out in the ghost train at Luna Park funfair. The fire was blamed on an electrical fault. Luna Park has closed, been rebuilt and has since reopened several times.

☆ **THE BIKIE SHOOTOUT**. On 2 September 1984, two motorbike gangs—the Comancheros and the Bandidos—had a shootout in the carpark of the Viking Tavern, Milperra, in which seven people were killed and 21 wounded. After a 332-day trial, nine gang members were found guilty of murder and 21 of manslaughter.

☆ **THE STRATHFIELD MASSACRE**. On 17 August 1991, Wade Frankum, a taxi driver, stabbed a 15-year-old girl to death in Strathfield shopping plaza and then shot dead six other people before turning the gun on himself.

15
crime

*t*he city founded by convicts currently has 2300 convicts in its 11 jails and detention centres. Our biggest jail is Long Bay, which means that people convicted of serious crimes can say they are being sent to 'the Bay' just as they did some 200 years ago. Most are in for drug dealing or 'break, enter and steal'.

The crimes that get the publicity in Sydney are 'ram raids' (in which young men steal a fast car and use it to smash the window of a shop so they can steal the contents, usually clothes) and 'home invasions' (in which a group of men smash down the door of a home, tie up the inhabitants, who are often recently-arrived Asian people, and steal money and jewellery). But in reality, these don't happen often enough to make much impact on the overall statistics.

You've heard of the Police Royal Commission, constable?

Commission, sir? Is it a form of incentive payment?

The crime with which most Sydneysiders are familiar is burglary. A total of 53 000 Sydney homes were broken into during 1996—a rise of 21 per cent on the previous year. And more than 90 per cent of home thefts go unsolved. The areas where homes are most likely to be burgled are Canterbury-Bankstown and the inner city. The area with the worst record for heroin dealing is Cabramatta, and—not necessarily by coincidence—it also has one of the highest rates of housebreaking.

But Sydney is not a dangerous city by world standards. Our murder rate of 2 per 100 000 citizens compares favourably with the rate of 50 per 100 000 achieved by Atlanta, the last Olympic city. But violent crime is rising. In 1996, 25 per cent more assaults (muggings, rapes and fights) were reported to the police than in the previous year. The areas with the worst assault records were the outer western suburbs of Mount Druitt, Campbelltown, and Penrith, followed by the inner city and Kings Cross.

Overall, the suburbs that seem to be most affected by crime are Botany, Leichhardt, Marrickville, Redfern and Cabramatta.

Asked in early 1997 to explain why crime seemed to have risen so rapidly in recent years, the Police Commissioner, Peter Ryan, said police may have 'taken their eye off the ball' for a while because they were worried about the royal commission into police corruption. But that is another chapter . . .

16
the cops

S ydney's first police force was a band of 12 convicts called The Night Watch, appointed to
patrol the streets by Governor Phillip in 1790. They
were paid in rum and sentence remissions. Some
might say that the notion of criminals watching
criminals has been the theme of law enforcement in
Sydney ever since.

In May 1994, NSW parliament set up a royal
commission to investigate the police force. The
police commissioner at the time, Tony Lauer, said
it would be a waste of time because 'there is no
entrenched corruption in the police service today'.
Three years later, Judge James Wood reported that
corruption was 'systemic and entrenched', particularly in the inner Sydney area.

The corruption ranged from accepting free drinks
or the services of prostitutes to receiving millions of
dollars from drug dealers. The police engaged in
shakedowns, beatings, extortion, stealing money or
drugs they found during searches, planting evidence,
reselling drugs they had confiscated, tipping off
dealers, and hampering investigations to assist
organised crime.

Wood said corruption had flourished because of

the failure of management to properly supervise, the ineptitude of the Internal Affairs Branch, the failure to rotate police out of drug-related squads, and the minimal training in ethics and integrity. The police culture provided rewards for officers who refused to 'dob' on their mates, no matter how corrupt they were, and vicious punishment for those who did report corruption.

The corrupt police had a special language to cover their activities. 'A giggle' is a bribe; 'the laugh' is a weekly total collected from illegal establishments, to be shared among several officers; 'a spot' is a bribe of $100; 'a monkey' is $500; 'a gorilla' is $1000; 'whippy' is money found during a search of a suspect's home, to be divided among the searchers; 'a scrumdown' is a meeting of officers to co-ordinate their evidence before a trial; 'fitting up' means constructing a false case against someone; 'loading up' means planting false evidence; to 'verbal' someone is to invent a confession; 'rebirthing' means reconstructing a stolen car to hide its origins; and 'whale in the bay' is a warning to a colleague that he is under investigation.

The portrait of the typical Sydney cop that emerged during the inquiry is a man who is minimally educated; cynical or pessimistic about society;

constantly suspicious; politically and socially conservative, with a 'macho outlook that promotes sexism and glorifies the abuse of alcohol'; and prejudiced against Aboriginal people, gays and lesbians, people of non-English-speaking backgrounds, juveniles, and the intellectually or physically disabled. And these were the relatively honest cops. A separate study found that 48 per cent of male police and 41 per cent of female police drink alcohol at levels considered hazardous (compared with 16 per cent of men and 10 per cent of women in the general community). The rate of police dying from alcohol-induced liver disease is double that of the general population.

Commissioner Tony Lauer retired in 1996. In all, 1020 NSW cops resigned or were dismissed in the three years of the Royal Commission, out of a total force of 13 000. Another 320 cops have been prosecuted. A British police officer, Peter Ryan, was appointed as the new commissioner. He promised to be 'vigilant and determined to break and remove toxic systems that allow cancerous elements to persist', which suggests he has an alternative career in medicine, if not in poetry.

17
the crooks

*t*here was a time when the Sydney newspapers had to refer to the city's criminals in code. One was known as Mr Big, another as Mr Sin. Crime was dominated by a couple of PRIs (Prominent Racing Identities), several LSBs (Leading Sydney Businessmen) and more than a few CSPs (Corrupt Senior Police).

Mr Big specialised in extortion, Mr Sin ran prostitution and drugs, the PRIs fixed the races, the LSBs ran illegal gambling casinos, the CSPs not only took bribes but actually organised robberies. It was frustrating for readers, who couldn't help wondering: if these people were so well known to the journalists and the police, how come they never got arrested?

But those were the bad old days. In the 1980s, most of the PRIs and the LSBs got left in the shallows by much bigger fish who dealt in millions instead of the thousands that the LSBs were used to. And nobody dared to call the big fish criminals.

But at least we can now put some names to those codes. In June 1997, an inquest into the disappearance of a hit man named Christopher Dale Flannery provided a collective portrait of many of the key figures in Sydney crime over the past two decades.

After examining witnesses for three years, the State Coroner, Greg Glass, concluded that a former Senior Police Officer named Roger Rogerson was probably involved in Flannery's disappearance, and had 'the motive and the opportunity to do harm' to him. A standover man named Neddy Smith told the inquest: 'There was no way that Flannery would go missing or be murdered unless Rogerson had either given permission or done the job himself'.

On the day he disappeared, Flannery (also known as Mr Rent-A-Kill) was on his way to see a businessman named George Freeman, for whom he had worked as a bodyguard. Since Freeman has since died, he can be revealed as a Prominent Racing Identity. Among the witnesses who professed to know nothing about the disappearance was a businessman named Lennie McPherson. Since he has also died since giving his 'argumentative, cantankerous and belligerent' testimony, he can be revealed as Mr Big.

But what of Mr Sin? He did not appear in that inquest, although he was discussed in the Police Royal Commission. We can say, however, that a police report tabled in the South Australian parliament in the late 1970s referred to a Sydney businessman named Abe Saffron who was involved in nightclubs, massage parlours, hotels and drug trafficking, and that Saffron has since spent three years in jail for conspiring to defraud the taxation department.

18
the power structure

*j*ust 200 years ago, the governors of New South Wales were absolute dictators—appointed by the British Government but effectively beyond its control. From his arrival in January 1788, Governor Arthur Phillip had the power to order the flogging, jailing or execution of anyone in NSW.

Although law courts were soon established, the governors kept their power for the first 36 years of the colony's existence. Then it was modified slightly by the appointment of a Legislative Council—seven men who were supposed to help the governor make the key decisions. After a lot of lobbying, the British Government agreed in 1842 to expand the council to 36, of whom 12 were appointed by the governor and 24 were elected by male settlers who owned land. The council was able to pass laws, but if the governor didn't like the laws, he could dissolve the council and send his own bills off to be ratified by Britain.

In 1856, NSW finally got an elected parliament, in the form of a 54-member Legislative Assembly (voted in by property-owners) and a 21-member Legislative Council (nominated by the governor) which would 'review' the decisions of the elected house. British troops, who had enforced the governor's will, were withdrawn in 1870. Compulsory voting was extended to all white males in 1858 and to women in 1902. Aboriginal people were not included until 1962.

In 1901, NSW ceased to be a colony of Britain and became a state within a nation called Australia (with Sydney as the state capital). That meant the state government lost the power to raise an army or to impose income taxes on its citizens, but retained power over education, law enforcement, health, transport and the environment. The national government is based in Canberra, about 300 km southwest of Sydney.

Since the 1860s, the most powerful person in NSW has been the premier, elected by the Legislative Assembly. There is still a governor who, in theory, is chosen by the monarch in Britain, but in reality, the Queen's office just 'rubber stamps' the recommendation of the premier who happens to be in power when a governor retires. The governor retains the power to dismiss the premier if he or she breaks the law, and then to call an election, but in the 20th century governors spent most of their time opening fetes. They did at least get to live in a gothic mansion built in Sydney's Botanic Gardens in 1845, but even that privilege disappeared in 1996, when the new governor said he'd prefer to live in his own home in the suburbs, and the NSW government took the opportunity to open the big house to the people.

The Government of NSW means the political party which has the largest number of members in the Legislative Assembly. The Assembly has 99 members elected for four year terms. The majority party leader becomes premier and appoints 20 ministers from among the elected party members. Each minister runs a department staffed by public servants. The Legislative Council (also called the Upper House) has 42 members, elected for eight year terms. The Council is regarded as a good place to get some sleep. Sydney's citizens also get to vote for the members of their local council, which has such functions as collecting the garbage, fixing the roads, and approving new buildings. The suburbs of Sydney are grouped into 42 local councils.

The legal system is independent of the government (although it passes the laws and appoints the judges). Minor charges (driving, assault, petty theft etc) are dealt with by magistrates in Local Courts (which also sit as Coroner's Courts, Children's Courts and Licensing Courts). More serious cases go before judges in the District Court, while the biggest issues are handled by judges and juries in the Supreme Court (which also handles appeals against lower court decisions). The ultimate court of appeal is the High Court in Canberra.

Of the people charged each year before Local Courts, about 87 per cent are found guilty and of these, 60 per cent are punished with a fine. Of the people charged in District and Supreme Courts, 75 per cent are found guilty, and 54 per cent of these are sent to prison.

19
the pollies

*P*olitics in NSW, as in the rest of Australia, operates under what is, in effect, a two-party system. On one side is the Labor Party which originated last century as the representative of the underdog. On the other side is the Liberal Party, traditionally the representative of big business, in coalition with the National Party, traditionally the representative of big farmers. There are also a few independents and members of tiny parties in NSW parliament to make the game more interesting.

Past Labor premiers of NSW whose names still echo in political discourse are:

☆ **JACK LANG**, known as 'the big fella', who was dismissed in 1932 by the governor because Lang's government appeared unable to pay state debts;

☆ **WILLIAM McKELL**, who refused in 1945 to accept the British Government's appointment of an Englishman to become the new governor and persuaded it to appoint an Australian. In 1947, McKell was himself appointed as Governor-General of Australia.

☆ **NEVILLE WRAN**, a social reformer (homosexuality was decriminalised during his term in office) and the initiator of so many grand projects—such as the Darling Harbour redevelopment, the monorail and the tunnel under Sydney Harbour—that he was described as having 'an edifice complex'. He retired in 1986 after ten years in office.

The tough school that is the NSW Labor Party also produced **Paul Keating**, who became Australia's Treasurer in 1982 and its Prime Minister between 1991 and 1996. He led the (so far unfinished) push for Australia to sever its ties with the British monarchy and become a republic.

Past Liberal premiers whose names still echo in political discourse are:

☆ **ROBERT ASKIN**, who presided over a period of intense development of Sydney in the late 1960s which meant the loss of many historic buildings. Askin was widely believed to be corrupt (accused of accepting bribes to protect illegal casinos and payments to award knighthoods).

☆ **NICK GREINER**, who resigned in 1992 after being accused of offering a public service job to a political opponent to get him out of parliament. The Supreme Court later found he had not acted corruptly.

☆ **JOHN FAHEY**, best known for making a
  mighty leap into the air on the night in 1993
  when Sydney was awarded the Olympic
  Games. Fahey was voted out in 1995 but went
  on to become Finance Minister in the national
  government in Canberra.

In 1995, the Labor Party was elected into government in NSW. The premier's position was filled
by **Bob Carr,** a former journalist and union research
officer with a passion for American politics (he
belongs to The Chester A Arthur Society, which
holds trivia quizzes about obscure US vice presi-
dents). He wants to be remembered for the amount
of national park space his government has declared.

Bob Carr's best-known Cabinet colleagues are:

☆ **MICHAEL EGAN**, the Treasurer, loathed by
  the party's left wing because of his wish to
  privatise some government agencies.

☆ **ANDREW REFSHAUGE**, the Health Minister,
  who has created debate over plans to move
  hospitals from the inner city to needier outlying
  areas.

☆ **MICHAEL KNIGHT**, the minister responsible
  for making sure the Olympics run smoothly,
  who is sometimes accused of megalomania.

The Leader of the Opposition in the NSW parliament is **Peter Collins**. He favours Australia
becoming a republic, which puts him at odds with
his Liberal colleagues who are in power in
Canberra.

20
big business

Of Australia's 100 biggest companies, 57 are based in Sydney, and together they earn revenue of $193 billion a year.

The biggest Sydney-based businesses are, from the top:

☆ **WOOLWORTH'S**, the shopping chain, $14.29 billion annual revenue and 94 600 employees.

☆ **NEWS CORPORATION**, Rupert Murdoch's media octopus, $14.27 billion annual revenue and 26 500 employees.

☆ **AMP**, an insurance and investment company that started in 1849 as the Australian Mutual Provident Society, $11.08 billion annual revenue and 11 100 employees.

☆ **THE COMMONWEALTH BANK**, $9.06 billion annual revenue and 36 000 employees.

☆ **WESTPAC**, founded in 1817 as the Bank of NSW, $8.56 billion annual revenue and 31 400 employees.

☆ **QANTAS**, Australia's national airline, $7.74 billion annual revenue

How to embarrass a company director

Mr Wetherby-Smythe, your mother dropped this off. She said she's run out of Nutella, so it's Vegemite today.

and 29 600 employees.

☆ **CSR**, a manufacturer of building materials, $6.38 billion annual revenue and 23 500 employees.

☆ **MITSUBISHI AUSTRALIA**, an importer of cars and equipment, $5.4 billion annual revenue and less than 200 employees.

☆ **BORAL**, a manufacturer of building materials, $5 billion annual revenue and 21 700 employees.

☆ **TNT**, a road and rail transportation company, $4.3 billion annual revenue and 36 300 employees.

So when the politicians say they are listening to 'the big end of town', that's who they mean.

21
the rich

*i*n the 1996 census, some 90 000 Sydney people or two per cent of the adult population reported that they were earning more than $70 000 a year. They tended to live on the upper north shore (Killara, Mosman and St Ives) and the eastern suburbs (Edgecliff, Bellevue Hill and Vaucluse). The financial magazine *BRW* produces an annual list of Australia's richest people. Of the 200 individuals and families listed in 1997, 84 live in Sydney, and they have a combined wealth of $17.4 billion.

Sydney's five wealthiest people are:

☆ **KERRY PACKER**, Australia's richest man, who has at least three Sydney homes—mansions at Bellevue Hill and Palm Beach and a flat in Elizabeth Bay—but spends about half the year in Britain (pursuing his passion for polo) and America (pursuing his passion for gambling). His fortune of $3.9 billion comes from interests in the Nine television network, casinos, magazines and the stock market. *BRW* estimated that during 1996, Packer earned $1.6 million a day.

☆ **FRANK LOWY**, boss of Westfield Holdings, which develops shopping centres in Australia and the US. He arrived as a penniless Czech immigrant in the 1950s and his first job was driving a delivery truck. Wealth: $1.4 billion.

☆ **HARRY TRIGUBOFF**, boss of the Meriton Group, which mass-produces cheap houses. Of Russian background, he reached Sydney at the age of 14 and first worked in his family's textile business. Wealth: $1.2 billion.

☆ **JOHN FAIRFAX**, who runs rural newspapers and radio stations. Wealth: $670 million, shared with his brother Timothy.

☆ **FRANCO BELGIORNO-NETTIS**, who owns the Transfield construction group, which built the Sydney Harbour Tunnel. Wealth: $500 million.

Sydney's richest woman is **Imelda Roche**, who runs the worldwide Nutrimetics cosmetics company with her husband Bill. She has to get by on a fortune of $216 million.

22
the poor

*t*he 1996 census showed nearly a million Sydney people over 15—that's a third of the total number—had a weekly income of less than $200.

The poorest areas in Sydney, as revealed by the census, are the inner suburbs of Redfern, Waterloo and Zetland, and the outer western suburbs of Villawood, Granville and Claymore.

According to a 1997 study by the Centre for Population and Urban Research at Monash University, some 28 per cent of Sydney people are dependent on welfare, with 11 per cent receiving the age pension, 4.3 per cent receiving the dole, 3.1 per cent receiving a disability allowance and 2.1 per cent receiving a single parent benefit.

That study suggests that 35 per cent of Sydney's children are in households that receive the maximum rate of family payment from the Federal Government—a grant of $96 every two weeks for each child under 12, and more for children between 13 and 15 years. The grant goes to families where all adults are unemployed or to working people whose family conditions may put the children at risk of deprivation. To get the grant, a family with one child must have an income less than $23 300.

The worst affected area in Sydney is Auburn, where two in every three children under the age of 15 are in families which get the payment—39 per cent qualify because the parents are on some form of welfare, and 21 per cent because the family income is deemed by the Department of Social Security to be low enough to warrant assistance.

But at least those welfare recipients have homes. The Federal Government has estimated that beneath that layer of poverty, there are 20 000 homeless adults in Sydney and 12 000 homeless people aged between 12 and 21, otherwise known as 'street kids'. The Sydney City Mission is the main source of help. Every year it picks up and feeds some 45 000 homeless people in Sydney, and it has 650 beds available on any given night, which is not nearly enough.

23
the communities

*W*ith more than 100 different national groups, as well as groupings based on wealth, occupation, sexual preference, and sporting loyalties, Sydney is a city of communities.

Sometimes the members are geographically scattered, coming together only on occasions when they want to celebrate their group identity—such as St Patrick's Day, the Sydney Gay & Lesbian Mardi Gras or Chinese New Year. Sometimes the community members live close by each other, forming what might be called ghettoes in less flexible societies but which are called Unique Shopping Opportunities in ours.

Here's where to find some of Sydney's smaller communities:

☆ **FILIPINO.** One of the fastest-growing immigrant groups, Filipinos are settling mainly in Fairfield and Blacktown, outer western suburbs.

☆ **GREEK.** The first Greeks in Sydney were seven convicts transported for piracy in 1829. More than 200 000 Greeks migrated to Australia between the 1940s and the 1970s, but more went to Melbourne than to Sydney. Those who landed here are famous for running cafes and milk bars in outer suburbs and country towns across the state. But the inner western suburb of Marrickville is still a Greek heartland (around St Nicholas Greek Orthodox church), with the Hellenic Bakery, Global Foods and TIM Products offering Greek ingredients on a gargantuan scale.

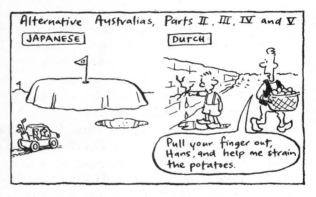

✫ **INDONESIAN**. Because Indonesia sends many students to Sydney, this community has tended to settle in the southeastern suburbs of Randwick, Kensington and Kingsford, within easy reach of the University of NSW. You're bound to find a decent *nasi rames* in the blocks between 100 and 500 Anzac Parade.

✫ **JAPANESE**. The Japanese tend to be temporary visitors to Sydney but they have a growing presence in the lower north shore, marked particularly by the rise of noodle shops in Neutral Bay and the fabulous Tokyo Mart in Northbridge Plaza.

✫ **JEWISH**. Jews have been worshipping together in Sydney since 1817, when a Jewish burial society was officially formed. In the first census in 1828, 95 people ticked the box for Judaism. The 1996 census put the NSW total at 32000. After World War Two, many Jews of middle European background settled in the eastern stretch from Bondi through Dover Heights to Rose Bay. For kosher meat, pastries, groceries and wine, the triangle of Hall and O'Brien Streets and Glenayr Avenue, Bondi is bound to prove productive.

✫ **KOREAN**. This community has congregated around the southern suburb of Campsie, with food stores and restaurants stretching along Beamish Street (between 100 and 400). They call it the Seoul of Sydney.

☆ **LEBANESE**. About 105 000 Sydney people or
3.5 per cent of the population speak Arabic at
home, and most of these came from Lebanon.
Lebanese Christians, who started arriving in
Australia in the 1840s, tend to live near the
Maronite Church in Redfern and run
restaurants along Cleveland Street. The
Muslims, who arrived after Lebanon's civil war
got worse in the mid 1970s, live in the
southwestern suburbs of Canterbury,
Bankstown and Lakemba, where there is a
major mosque.

☆ **NEW ZEALANDERS**. According to the Sydney
stereotype, New Zealanders (who need no visas
to enter Australia) settle around Bondi Beach,
while Maori transvestites settle into Kings
Cross and stand around William Street late at
night. In fact, New Zealanders live everywhere.

☆ **PORTUGUESE**. These people, and their
colonial colleagues the Brazilians, have settled in
the inner western suburb of Petersham (but tend
to do their weekend picnicking around Bronte
Beach). A stroll along the early numbers of New
Canterbury Road reveals a variety of charcoal
chicken joints, bakeries, delis, butcheries and
liquor shops devoted to the delights of the lower
Iberian peninsula. Just off New Canterbury
Road, at 82 Audley Street, is Gloria's Cafe,
where swarthy men sit and chat over cigarettes
and strong black coffees called *bica*.

☆ **SOUTH AMERICAN**. About 45 000 Sydney
people or 1.5 per cent of the population speak
Spanish at home. Most came from South
American countries, and headed south and west
when they arrived in Sydney. Result: Carniceria
los Rodriguez (a butchery which also sells
sweet potato jelly) at 485 Hume Highway,
Yagoona, and some interesting Chilean,
Uruguayan and Argentinian delis and cake
shops around Spencer, Barbara and Nelson
Streets, Fairfield. There's also an area
nicknamed 'Little Spain' in the city centre near
the corner of Liverpool and George Streets.

☆ **THAI**. Judging by the number of Thai
restaurants that opened in Sydney suburbs
during the 1980s, you'd imagine there had been
a huge influx of immigrants from Thailand. In
fact, the numbers were in the hundreds rather
than the thousands, and the restaurants are
mostly run by Vietnamese or Chinese people
who spotted a trend in public taste.

☆ **TURKISH**. The Muslim community from
Turkey tends to live around the western
suburbs of Canterbury or Auburn, which has a
major mosque. Some intriguing pastry and
sweet shops can be found in the lower numbers
of Auburn Road. Turks also run restaurants
around Surry Hills, where they have started a
fad for soft, chewy *pide* bread, often served
stuffed with spicy meats (but not pork).

24
the Chinese

*t*he first Chinese immigrant to Australia that we know of (because it's entirely possible that explorers from China were visiting this continent a thousand years ago) was Mak Sai Ying. Born in Canton in 1798, he sailed into Sydney voluntarily in 1818, at a time when most immigrants were arriving under compulsion. He bought land at Parramatta, changed his name to John Shying, and married an Englishwoman. By 1829 he was running the Lion Inn in Parramatta and his descendants live there still.

Chinese immigration increased hugely after the discovery of gold west of the Blue Mountains in 1851. Australia was called 'New Gold Mountain' in China, where California had been known as 'Gold Mountain'. By 1861 there were 38 000 Chinese people in Australia (3.3 per cent of the population—the

highest proportion there has ever been). Of this group, only 11 were women. When the gold ran out, most returned to China but some stayed to start market gardens and restaurants. By early in the 20th century,

Australians were comfortably dining out on sweet and sour pork, chicken chow mein and prawn chop suey.

Sydney's most famous Chinese citizen in the 19th century was Quong Tart, who arrived as a child in 1859 and started a tea and silk importing business in 1874. His tearooms became Sydney's most fashionable meeting place and were remarked upon by the visiting writer Robert Louis Stevenson. Quong Tart was killed by robbers in his tearoom in 1903 and is buried in Sydney's enormous Rookwood cemetery.

Anti-Asian prejudice was the primary motive for the first act passed by the Australian Federal Parliament in 1901, a piece of legislation that came to be known as the White Australia Policy. Chinese immigration and investment were minimal after this time until the policy was formally ended by Gough Whitlam's government in 1973. The figures rose rapidly again after Britain agreed to hand back Hong Kong to the Chinese government.

Nowadays some 115 000 Sydney people—4 per cent of the population—speak Chinese at home, although many of these are from Vietnam rather than China. There are Chinese communities in Burwood in the inner west and Chatswood in the northern suburbs, where many of the wealthier Chinese live.

Sydney also has a thriving Chinatown around Dixon Street in the CBD, where yum cha has become one of the city's weekend rituals.

25
the Italians

*b*y a small stretch, you could argue that the city of Sydney owes its existence to an Italian. James Mario Matra—born in America, apparently of Italian origin—was a midshipman on James Cook's ship the *Endeavour* when it landed at Botany Bay in 1770. Back in England, he became a passionate advocate for its development as a colony. Matra made the extravagant argument that 'If a colony from Britain was established in the large Tract of Country, & if we were at war with Holland or Spain, we might very powerfully annoy either state from our new settlement'. When this was greeted with scepticism, he added an after-thought that prisoners might be sent to New South Wales: 'They cannot fly from the country, they have no temptation to theft, and they must work or starve'.

Italians were among the many Europeans who headed for Sydney when the gold rush began in 1851, and in 1881 their numbers were boosted by 200 new arrivals who had taken part in a failed experiment to set up a perfect society in New Guinea. The NSW government said it would only help them to become citizens if they didn't live together: 'The customs of the country and other circumstances render it undesirable, indeed almost impossible, for them to settle down together in one locality. Even if this were practicable, it would not be for their own good to do so'.

After World War Two, Italians became the main non-English-speaking group in the Australian government's assisted immigration program. Some 500 000 Italians migrated between 1947 and 1980, and more settled in Sydney than in any other capital. They can take credit for the transformation of this city over the past three decades into a Mediterranean culture devoted to coffee, pasta and the pursuit of pleasure. Australians of Italian origin are now widely dispersed through the suburbs, but there is still a community clustered around Leichhardt and Haberfield. Foodies make pilgrimages to Leichhardt to the A C Butchery, 174 Marion Street and Norton Street Market, 55 Norton Street.

Three of Sydney's great business success stories are men who arrived penniless from Italy in the early 1950s: Franco Belgiorno-Nettis, who runs the Transfield building group which built the Sydney Harbour tunnel and who, in 1997, had a fortune of half a billion dollars; Carlo Salteri, whose company makes ships and military equipment and whose personal fortune is around $400 million; and Beppi Polese, who started the influential Beppi's restaurant in East Sydney, and who now owns real estate all over town.

26
the Vietnamese

*b*etween 1975 and 1990, 140 000 Vietnamese people arrived in Australia, many of them in leaky boats with the few possessions they could grab as they hurried to escape a government whose political approach they did not share. Australia accepted them as refugees because of a guilty conscience about its involvement in the Vietnam War, fighting on America's side.

Many Vietnamese were settled in migrant hostels in western Sydney, gradually moving to live and work in nearby suburbs. Nowadays, Sydney has about 50 000 residents who were born in Vietnam.

The stereotype is that most of them live in Cabramatta, which has been nicknamed Vietnamatta. The reality is that the Vietnamese tend to have their homes at Fairfield and Bankstown (notable for the restaurants Minh, Pasteur and Pho An), even if their businesses are in Cabramatta (which also has many residents from China, Burma and Cambodia).

The stereotype also portrays Cabramatta as a centre of violence and drug dealing, because of the activities of teenage gangs. There is certainly a crime problem, but that's unlikely to impinge on the visitor who takes a 45-minute train ride from central Sydney and strolls down John Street on a Saturday morning. That's the time when the shops are overflowing—not just with fresh foodstuffs unobtainable elsewhere in Sydney, but with bargains in homewares, fabrics and dressmaking materials.

Some conservative politicians, who would like all of Australia to look the same, are alarmed by the notion that stepping into Cabramatta is like being transported to a town in South East Asia. Most Sydney people find the opportunity stimulating. They tend to agree with the sign on the Pailau Gate at the entrance to Cabramatta's Freedom Plaza which says: 'The world is for us to share and to respect'.

27
gays and lesbians

*i*t's estimated that some 400 000 people in Sydney prefer to have sex with others of the same gender, which makes Sydney the second queerest city in the world, after San Francisco.

Lesbianism has never been illegal here, but sex between men was a criminal offence until the state parliament voted to decriminalise it in 1984. Many members of the queer community like to celebrate their group identification by living and playing in two areas: around Oxford Street, Darlinghurst in the inner east and around King Street, Newtown in the inner west. There's also a small lesbian community further west in Leichhardt, which revels in the nickname Dykeheart.

The major gay and lesbian celebration of the year is the Mardi Gras, a parade held in late February preceded by a month of cultural events. The Mardi Gras started in 1978 as a small protest march against oppression but has grown into a multi-million dollar festival which now attracts straights and queers, tourists and locals alike.

The stretch of Oxford Street just east and west of Taylor Square is nicknamed The Pink Precinct. The Albury Hotel and the Oxford Hotel are the most convivial gay pubs, while lesbians tend to meet upstairs at the Exchange Hotel or on the top floor of Kinselas on Sunday nights. The most glamorous nightclubs in this strip are DCM and The Midnight Shift.

In King Street, the gay pub is the Newtown Hotel, while lesbians like the Bank Hotel. On the edge of Newtown is the Imperial Hotel, Erskineville, which has regular Abba nights. Scenes from the movie *Priscilla: Queen of the Desert* were filmed there. And the Leichhardt Hotel on Balmain Road is the meeting place for the formidable cult called Dykes on Bikes. *The Sydney Star Observer* newspaper is one way to keep up with community news.

Not entirely by coincidence, Sydney has the highest rate of AIDS-related deaths in Australia— seven per 100 000 people compared with a national rate of four. Australia's biggest HIV/AIDS charity, the Bobby Goldsmith Foundation, is based here.

28
style

*C*asual is the word. The bumper sticker that says 'I'd rather be sailing' sums up the Sydney attitude. The sticker could equally say 'I'd rather be drinking coffee in a street cafe'. If traditional Australia was the land of meat pies and beer, then modern Sydney is the land of focaccia and cappuccino. We've got the Mediterranean weather, and in the past 30 years we've developed the attitude to match.

Being punctual for a social engagement means arriving within an hour of the appointed time—after that, you're starting to look a bit late. Socialising with friends means going out for yum cha or coming round for a barbecue rather than sitting down for a dinner party. Dressing up means ironing your jeans. I can't think of a single restaurant in Sydney these days that requires men to wear a jacket and tie for dinner, although that rule may survive in some of the stuffier clubs. A few pubs refuse admission to people wearing thongs.

Everyone uses mobile phones. Those Sydney-siders who got annoyed in the early 1990s when they saw people talking on mobile phones in restaurants are now doing it themselves.

Tipping means leaving ten per cent in a restaurant if you *really* liked the service, and about five per cent otherwise. A dollar is nice for someone who carries your bags in a hotel, but if you don't have the change, don't worry about it. In taxis, it's common for the driver to tip the passenger by rounding the fare down to the nearest dollar if it's five or ten cents over. Passengers sometimes round the fare up to the nearest dollar if the driver hasn't been too unpleasant during the journey, earning themselves an 'Oh thanks, have a good day'.

Sydney has a small way to go yet before it becomes fully Mediterranean. The residual Anglo Saxonism means most of us have not yet discovered the advantages of siesta, late night dining, and living in the central business district (which tends to be dead at weekends). But those advances cannot be far away.

29

tourist stuff

*i*t's hard for Sydney people to accept that our major role in life these days is entertaining visitors. Once upon a time, Australia's biggest moneymaker from overseas was wool, most of it shipped out of Sydney. Now the nation's biggest earner is tourism, which adds $14 billion a year to the Australian economy and creates more than 200 000 jobs. Sydney does most of the work for that money.

Of the 3.7 million people who visit Australia each year, more than two million spend time in Sydney. About a third of the foreigners who holiday in Sydney come from Japan. The next most eager arrivals come from New Zealand, Britain, the USA, South Korea and Taiwan. But the biggest spenders per head are visitors from Germany, Indonesia, Scandinavia, Canada, Hong Kong and Malaysia, so we have to figure out ways to attract more of them. The lowest spenders are New Zealanders.

Eight of the ten favourite attractions in Australia—as nominated to the Bureau of Tourism Research by

What brings you back to Sydney Harbour?

The glamour, the nightlife, the world class seafood...

Wilcox

overseas visitors—are in Sydney (the other two are Uluru in Central Australia, and the Barrier Reef in Queensland). The attractions most remembered by departing visitors are the shopping, the beaches, the Opera House, the Harbour, The Rocks, Sydney Tower, Darling Harbour and the Blue Mountains.

So far, we've only talked about foreigners. Sydney is also the drawcard for visitors from elsewhere in Australia. Australians spend $32 billion a year travelling in their own country. Nearly a third of all nights spent away from home are in Sydney. The major place of origin for visitors to Sydney is 'elsewhere in NSW', followed by Victoria.

Sydney accommodates these visitors in more than 300 hotels and motels, with 67 000 beds, which earn some $832 million a year. Many more rooms are being created to meet expected demand during the Olympics in the year 2000. Just don't ask what happens to all that space when the Games are over.

30
the reality tour, part one

g'day, kon-nichi-wah, and have a nice day, blokes and sheilas, mee nah sun and guys and gals. Welcome aboard our great big smelly bus for the Realists' Tour of Sydney, the journey of discovery for travellers who want to throw aside the rose-coloured glasses. I'm your designated driver and guide. Today, we're going to hit the sights the other tours don't dream of reaching.

The others will drag you round the Harbour and Bondi Beach and the wildlife parks. Not us. This tour is not for the faint of heart. We'll show you Australia's top suburb for sleaze. We'll show you the cheapest house in Sydney, and some of the most absurdly expensive. We'll stand where two bikie gangs set out to massacre each other one quiet Sunday afternoon. We'll drink a beer in a club that outdrinks any other club in the world. And we'll pass through some of the unhealthiest suburbs in Australia. But don't panic, because as soon as we enter the danger zone, oxygen masks will drop down from the console above your head. And when we pass Sydney's two nuclear reactors, you can relax in the knowledge that our coach is lead-lined.

There'll be no koala fondling on this trip. And the furthest we'll go into the picturesque eastern suburbs will be number 181 Birriga Road, Bellevue Hill, a drab flat where the English comedian Tony Hancock committed suicide in 1968 while visiting Sydney to make a TV series. That event symbolised the end of the era when overseas entertainers who had failed everywhere else could come to Australia and still make a few bucks. Hancock's suicide note said: 'Things seemed to go wrong too many times'. Nowadays, of course, Sydney gets suicidal entertainers at the *peak* of their careers.

Let's climb off the bus here in Darlinghurst Road, Kings Cross, so we can study the array of imaginative signs for establishments such as Stripperama, The Pink Pussycat, Love Machine and Playbirds. These are interesting enough in themselves, but many of the facades in this street conceal other services. There are places behind these doors called 'shooting galleries' where heroin addicts can buy syringe kits and rent rooms to inject themselves in peace. The 1997 report of the Royal Commission into the NSW Police Service recommended that these shooting galleries be legalised, but the state government is unlikely to agree.

This area is known to the police of Sydney as Goldenhurst, because of its reputation as a gold mine for cops who are willing to look the other way. It also features in the name of a famous police interrogation method—the Darlo drop—in which a group of cops throw a suspect up into the air and let him fall to the floor. This technique was pioneered at Darlinghurst police station.

As we stroll around, the male members of our party may find themselves being asked 'Like a girl, love?' by young women on the street. It's OK—prostitution is legal in Sydney as long as the workers don't hang around outside churches, schools and private homes. There are brothels in Liverpool, Tusculum and Hargrave Streets. Male prostitutes hang round the southern end of Darlinghurst Road in an area called The Wall. This runs next to Sydney's old jail, where 67 people were executed between 1840 and 1908. Nowadays the old Jail is an art school.

If we wander down Victoria Street, we can look at some 1970s apartment blocks and wonder which of them has the body of Juanita Nielsen under its foundations. She was a campaigner against the demolition of old houses in the street until she disappeared on 4 July 1975.

Now let's drop off for a quick cuppa at the Cosmo Coffee Lounge, 95 Darlinghurst Road, where as recently as 1996 the Royal Commission filmed drug deals taking place. Supposedly, packets of heroin and cocaine were hidden in the sugar bowls, so watch what you put in your coffee. Then join me back on the bus . . .

31
the reality tour, part two

*n*ow our bus heads out of the CBD through Newtown and on to the Princes Highway, where we make a left turn into Barden Street, Tempe, to view the cheapest house in Sydney. In a town that has the highest home prices in Australia and where half the houses cost more than $260 000, this place received huge publicity in the early 1990s by selling for just $40 000. It's a little wooden number, somewhat in need of renovation, but the explanation for the price lies in the setting—a car wrecker's yard down one end of the street, a rubbish dump at the other, and right overhead, the comforting sound of almost all of the planes that use Sydney Airport.

We're seeing that house by way of contrast with our next destination, somewhat further south, past the airport (hated by more than 50 per cent of Sydney's population since the opening of a third runway increased the noise level). We are driving into an enclave called Sylvania Waters where the houses show what you can build or buy if you're a successful real estate agent or used car salesman or dealer in substances some police might frown upon. The area was developed as recently as 1963 from a set of oyster farms, and the idea was that every homebuyer would be able to park two cars in the garage out front and two boats on the canal out back. The section called James Cook Island could easily be mistaken for Venice or the French Quarter of New Orleans or the set of *Gone With The Wind*—sometimes all three at once. Cherubs, columns, fountains, pediments, iron lace and man-icured lawns go together to make a style called 'ABBA Architecture', which stands for All Bloody Balustrades and Arches. This is the home territory of Laurie and Noelene from the early 1990s TV series about Sydney life that fascinated the British and embarrassed Australians.

Now we head west, across some of the city's most polluted waterways, and on to our shining symbol of the atomic age—Lucas Heights Nuclear Research Station. When he opened the first of the two reactors here in 1958, Australia's then prime minister, Sir Robert Menzies, said there would soon be many more reactors to provide Australia's energy needs. Somehow it didn't work out that way. Indeed, many local residents spend much of their time trying to get rid of the Lucas Heights facility, even though its main role is researching atomic energy for medical purposes.

We'll turn into Mendeleeff Road, which gives us the best view of the main reactor. Oh, dear, it looks as if it's been blocked off for security reasons. We're certainly proud to know that Australia has something worth keeping secret. And now up Henry Lawson Drive, named after some old poet, to the carpark of the Viking Tavern at 189 Beaconsfield Street, Milperra. This is one of Sydney's most historic battlegrounds. On 2 September 1984, warfare broke out here between two motorbike gangs, the Comancheros and the Bandidos. They fought with shotguns, rifles, machetes, baseball bats and spanners, and at the end, seven people were dead and 21 injured. We have time for a small beer, but please be careful what you say to the locals.

And now we're heading through Sydney's sickest suburbs. A report released in the mid 1990s declared that Fairfield and Bankstown had some of the highest rates of heart disease, cancer, strokes and respiratory disorders of any part of the city. Hold onto your oxygen masks now, we'll be clear of this in a couple of minutes.

Here on Woodville Road, you'll notice on our right one of the Seven Wonders of Sydney—a giant orange rock made of plaster, atop its own little Eiffel Tower, kindly contributed to the urban aesthetic by Rock Around The Block timber yard. You may gasp at this, but wait till we turn left onto the F4 freeway and pull over. It's breathtaking—a massive pink arrow in the middle of a wasteland, pointing into the ground and identifying The Centre of Sydney.

We're stopping briefly now to pick up another group of Realistic Travellers who have chosen to stay as close as they can to The Centre—in the Prospect Hotel/Motel, which is topped, as you can see, by Sydney's largest beer can. And now on to our next refreshment stop, the Blacktown Workers Club. We're visiting because this is the place that sells the most tap beer in the world. The 21 000 members and their guests get through more than a million litres of the amber fluid a year, more even than any beer hall in Germany. There are also hundreds of different poker machines to choose from, many at 10 cents a pull. Please be back in the bus by 2pm.

And off we go again. We're about to have a little picnic. Would you please de-coach at this time, and we'll sit by the Duck River at Clyde, gazing across to the Shell Oil Refinery, just up the road from Silverwater Prison and the navy's armaments depot. Notice the unique grey colour of the river and the complete absence of life forms. I would not advise dangling your feet in the water.

Let us return to the city centre now via the highlight of this tour—Parramatta Road, sometimes known as 'the magic mile after mile of motors'. The car yards and fast food stores along this famous stretch of highway compete for the uniqueness of their displays, designed to entice the discerning customer. Any rational person would make the journey from Parramatta to the city centre by Jetcat along the Parramatta River but we choose to do it the hard way—queuing for hours behind thousands of other angry drivers—because we want to get one final breath of the real Sydney.

You've had a special experience today, ladies and gentlemen, sampling parts of a great metropolis that are rarely seen, at least voluntarily, by its own citizens. We hope you'll return to your hometowns and spread the word that Sydney has nothing to hide.

32
the second city

*t*hese days, the only people who talk about Sydney-Melbourne rivalry are Melburnians, because Sydneysiders are so sure of their superiority they don't need to discuss it. But in the late 19th century, the rivalry was real and bitter, and for a while it looked as if Melbourne would win.

When the city to the south was founded in 1837, it was part of the empire of New South Wales, controlled from Sydney. In 1850, we let it go, generously allowing what was then called 'the Port Phillip district' to become a self-governing entity—the capital of a new colony called Victoria. In retrospect, that looked like a foolish gesture, because two years later gold was discovered in Victoria in far greater quantities than the gold discovered in NSW in 1851.

During the 1850s, the Victorian goldfields produced eight times as much gold as those in NSW. Melbourne attracted the fast money people from around the world. Australia's first stock exchange was set up there in 1865 (Sydney waited until 1871) and Melbourne's population numbers surged ahead of Sydney's. But Melbourne was hit much worse by the depression of 1890 as British investors reassessed their role in Australia and the flow of capital dried up. It never fully recovered. At the turn of the century, when the six states banded together to form a nation called Australia, Melbourne and Sydney both had populations approaching half a million.

From there, Sydney began to pull ahead. In 1986, at the peak of 1980s financial madness, turnover at Sydney's stock exchange totalled $44 million compared with $28 million at the Melbourne exchange.

But while Melbourne might have lost the financial advantage, it could still claim the cultural advantage for most of the 20th century. Lacking interesting views and clement weather, its citizens had to turn inwards, towards more intellectual and convivial pursuits. Bleak City prided itself on fostering Australia's best artists, writers and chefs, while Sydney just lazed at the beach.

Even this claim of cultural superiority had ceased to be true by the 1980s. Sydney leapt upon the popular art forms, opening a film and television school and becoming Australia's movie capital. All the TV networks based themselves here (although they tended to set their crime dramas in Victoria). The top writers moved here. And, transformed by a vast influx of immigrants, Sydney became the nation's gastronomic laboratory, with chefs

opening themselves to Asian influences while Melbourne stayed with French traditions.

In the 1990s, Victoria's hyperactive premier, Jeff Kennett, has been fighting back, offering all sorts of incentives to bring major events and major investment to Melbourne. He filched the motoring grand prix from Adelaide, and the Australian premiere of the musical 'Sunset Boulevard' from Sydney. Still, as Sydney people like to say, when you try so much harder, that just proves you're number two.

33
firsts

*b*eing Australia's original city, Sydney was bound to have produced the odd break-through. Here's a sampling.

☆ The world's first prepaid letter sheets, the forerunners of stamps, were introduced by the postmaster for the Sydney district on 1 November 1838.

☆ The world's first postage stamps with views (instead of portraits) were issued in January 1850 by the NSW postal service. The views were of sights around Sydney.

☆ Granny Smith apples started in the Eastwood garden of an English immigrant named Maria Smith. In the 1860s she threw some Tasmanian apple cores out her kitchen window, only to find that they were eventually turning into trees. Further breeding by her family through the late 19th century produced the durable green-skinned apple that went round the world.

☆ The second national park in the world opened south of Sydney in 1879, later called the Royal National Park. The first to open was Yellowstone in America, but it was not officially registered until after the Royal.

☆ Sydney led the way in trams: horse-drawn ones were introduced in 1879, followed by steam in 1879, then cable in 1886 and electric in 1890. The last tram in Sydney ran in 1961 between La Perouse and Randwick depot.

☆ Australia's first heavier-than-air flight was by the Sydney inventor Lawrence Hargrave on 12 November 1894, when he flew five metres into the air using four box kites at Stanwell Park, south of Sydney. The shapes of the kites he built were influential in the wing design of most early aeroplanes.

☆ Australia's first powered flight was made by Colin Defries on 9 December 1909 at Victoria Park racecourse in Sydney.

☆ Sydney was the first city in the world to appoint female police officers. It happened in 1915, when Lillian Armfield and Maude Rhodes joined the force, mainly with the role of protecting women and children.

☆ The Australian Crawl, the standard swimming stroke in Olympic competition, was developed by the Cavill family (father Fred, sons Arthur, Sydney and Richard) in Sydney pools in the 1910's.

☆ The world's first beauty contest in which competitors were judged in swimsuits was held at Sydney's Maroubra Beach on 18 February 1920. The winner was 14-year-old Edith Pickup of Manly. (The first Miss

America, chosen the following year, was 15.)

☆ The world's first heart pacemaker was made in Sydney and its first recorded use was in 1926 on a newborn baby at Crown Street Womens Hospital.

☆ The world's first milk bar opened in Martin Place in 1933, offering 'milk shakes' for four pence (extra for an egg yolk). The idea was taken to Britain by an Australian entrepreneur in 1935. In 1956, a Sydney police report called milk bars 'a breeding ground for delinquency'.

☆ The link between pregnant women contracting rubella (German measles) and blindness in their children was discovered in 1939 by a Sydney ophthalmologist, Dr Norman McAlister Gregg. Now women are routinely vaccinated against rubella.

☆ The first long service leave in the world—three months after 20 years service—was introduced by the NSW government in 1951.

☆ Australia's first commercial television was transmitted from Channel Nine, Sydney on 16 September 1956.

☆ The world's first official surf championships were held at Manly Beach in May 1964 and won by Bernard 'Midget' Farrelly, 19, from Dee Why.

☆ Microsurgery was pioneered by the Sydney surgeon Earl Owen, who replaced the amputated finger of a two-year-old child in

1968 and designed instruments now widely used in Europe.

☆ Dynamic lifter (a fertiliser made from dried chicken manure) was developed in 1971 by Norman Jennings of Sydney.

☆ Controlled crying (a technique for establishing a convenient sleeping pattern in infants) was developed by Dr Christopher Green, head of the Child Development Unit at Royal Alexandra Hospital in the mid 1970s. The idea is to leave the child crying a little longer each time it wakes in the night, so that it learns to put itself back to sleep. The system has been adopted in Britain, Germany and Japan.

☆ Australia's first saint is buried in St Joseph's Convent, North Sydney. Mary MacKillop founded the Josephite order of nuns in 1866, dedicated to the education of poor children in outback Australia. Pope John Paul II began the beatification process during his Sydney visit in 1995. Sydney is fond of her because she was accused of drunkenness.

34
stars

S ydney takes credit for Mel Gibson, even if he was born in America, because he trained at NIDA (the National Institute of Dramatic Art, near the University of NSW at Kensington) and because he made his first films here, notably the *Mad Max* series.

Tom Cruise and Nicole Kidman also belong to us, because she grew up here and in 1995 they paid $4.2 million for a three-storey apartment in Darling Point, which they occasionally visit.

Here are some of our other glitterati:

☆ **BANANAS IN PYJAMAS.** Plus, of course, the Teddies and the Rat in a Hat. Their short shows, made by ABC children's television at Gore Hill, earn millions from the TV stations of the world.

☆ **RAY BARRETT.** Brisbane born, Sydney-trained, he got roles as cops or thugs on British

TV during the 1960s and 70s, and now tends to play ocker dads in small Aussie films.

☆ **BRUCE BERESFORD.** He directed *The Adventures of Barry McKenzie* here, moved upmarket to make *Driving Miss Daisy* in Hollywood, and came home to direct *Paradise Road*.

☆ **BRYAN BROWN.** Here he was the rugged star of *Breaker Morant* and *A Town Like Alice*. Over there he made *Cocktail*, *FX* and *Gorillas in the Mist*.

☆ **RUTH CRACKNELL.** The doyenne of Sydney theatre and television, she's best known as the absent-minded mum in the sitcom *Mother and Son*.

☆ **JUDY DAVIS.** Perth-born, Sydney-trained (at NIDA with Mel Gibson), she became America's pre-eminent player of neurotic women, returning to live in Balmain and play similar roles in Aussie films.

☆ **KEN DONE.** A graphic artist from the advertising industry, he made millions in the 1980s designing colourful towels and bags for tourists, often with Sydney Harbour motifs. He is huge in Japan. Now he is concentrating on more serious painting.

☆ **JOHN FARNHAM.** Since his first hit single, *Sadie The Cleaning Lady*, in 1967, the 'King of Pop' has kept reviving his singing career with blockbuster albums, particularly

Whispering Jack in 1986 and *Chain Reaction* in 1990.

✰ **REG GRUNDY.** He's a creator of TV shows who started in Sydney with quizzes such as *Wheel of Fortune*, *The Price Is Right* and *Sale of the Century*, and moved on to soaps such as *The Restless Years*, *Sons and Daughters*, *Prisoner* and *Neighbours*. Then he repeated his success in Los Angeles. The Grundy company is now the largest packager of TV programs in the world, operating in 32 countries.

✰ **BRUCE GYNGELL.** The first talking-head to appear on Australian television in 1956, he went on to run the Seven Network here and several TV stations in Britain.

✰ **PAUL HOGAN.** The quintessential Sydney boy, he was working as a rigger on the Harbour Bridge when he won a TV talent quest in the early 1970s and went on to make cigarette commercials, his own top-rating comedy show, ads for Australian tourism in America and the film *Crocodile Dundee*. He moved to America and made a series of movie flops.

✰ **ROBERT HUGHES.** He's now America's most influential art critic and cultural commentator but he remembered his hometown well enough to write *The Fatal Shore*, the definitive tale of European settlement.

✰ **BILL HUNTER.** Though born in Melbourne, Bill Hunter is a Sydney acting institution, always available to play an ocker father (*Muriel's Wedding*) or an ocker bureaucrat (*Strictly Ballroom*).

☆ **MICHAEL HUTCHENCE.** Once known as the singer with INXS, he has moved far from his Perth upbringing and is now better known as an international hanger-around. When in Sydney, he hangs around Darlinghurst.

☆ **CLIVE JAMES.** Born in Kogarah, he became a journalist, critic and talk show host in Britain, where they think his wit is iconoclastically Australian.

☆ **DARE JENNINGS.** In 1986, he founded a line of teen clothing called Mambo, with designs based on surfing and scatology, and by 1996 he was selling $25 million worth of product in 20 countries.

☆ **BAZ LUHRMANN.** After directing *Strictly Ballroom* (with help from his partner, designer Catherine Martin) the pair went to Hollywood and made a hit out of *Romeo and Juliet*.

☆ **HUGH MACKAY.** He runs a sociological research company, and in the 1990s he became Australia's best-known commentator on the national psyche, via a column in *The Australian*, frequent radio appearances and a bestseller called *Reinventing Australia*.

☆ **ELLE MACPHERSON.** She's a top swimsuit model, now running businesses and acting in US films.

☆ **GARRY McDONALD.** Australia's top comic actor, he graduated from NIDA in 1967, worked in stage plays, and then created the world's clumsiest TV talk show host Norman Gunston and the world's most long-suffering son, Arthur in TV's *Mother and Son*.

☆ **MENTAL AS ANYTHING.** They were a 1980s rock band who went big with international hits *The Nips Are Getting Bigger* and *Live It Up*. The members—Reg Mombasa, Peter O'Doherty, Andrew 'Greedy' Smith and Martin Murphy (aka Martin Plaza)—keep returning to prominence with individual art and music projects.

☆ **MIDNIGHT OIL.** A rock band led by the environmentally-active Peter Garrett, their *Beds are Burning* has been rated one of the 500 most influential rock songs of all time by the US Rock and Roll Hall of Fame.

☆ **GEORGE MILLER.** Director of the Mad Max movies here, he went to America to make *The Witches of Eastwick*, and returned to make *Babe*.

☆ **JOHN NEWCOMBE.** A multiple Wimbledon winner in the early 1970s, 'Newk' became a tennis coach, commentator and sport adviser.

☆ **PHIL NOYCE.** He directed *Newsfront* here and then, under the name Phillip Noyce, became one of Hollywood's top action directors with *Patriot Games* and *The Saint*.

☆ **JOHN PILGER.** A troublemaking journalist and film-maker, he wrote *The Secret Country* about power and poverty in Australia. He now lives in London.

☆ **JOAN SUTHERLAND.** An opera soprano, she won the Sydney Sun aria competition in 1949 at the age of 23 and went on to earn the name La Stupenda round the world. She now lives mainly in Switzerland.

☆ **JACK THOMPSON.** Blonder than Bryan Brown, he's done rugged roles here in *Breaker Morant* and *The Sum of Us*, and gone to Hollywood for *Broken Arrow* and *Midnight in the Garden of Good and Evil.*

☆ **PETER WEIR.** He directed *Picnic at Hanging Rock* and *Gallipoli* here, then *Witness*, *Dead Poets Society* and *Green Card* in Hollywood.

☆ **JAMES WOLFENSOHN.** A Sydney University law graduate and Olympic fencer for Australia, he's now President of the World Bank in New York, which makes him the world's second most influential Australian (after Rupert Murdoch).

☆ **ROGER WOODWARD.** If the movie *Shine* hadn't made a star out of David Helfgott, his ancient rival Roger Woodward would have been Australia's best-known international pianist. Trained in Sydney, he's played Chopin everywhere and now lives mainly in London.

35
heroes

Sydneysiders have a habit of admiring sporting efforts as much as intellectual or humanitarian achievements, so the local products we remember with reverence are a curious mixture.

☆ **JACK BRABHAM**. Born in Hurstville, he was the world champion car racing driver three times during the 1960s, winning 14 Grand Prix, sometimes in cars he designed himself.

☆ **JIMMY CARRUTHERS**. He became the world bantamweight boxing champion in 1952 and retired undefeated in 1954, running a vegetarian food shop until his death in 1991.

☆ **VICTOR CHANG**. He was the pioneer of heart transplant surgery in Australia and his team at St Vincent's Hospital, Darlinghurst, performed more than 300 heart transplants during the 1980s. He was shot dead in a bungled robbery attempt in 1991.

☆ **ANDREW 'BOY' CHARLTON**. He was an Olympic swimming gold medallist in 1924, aged 17. The Domain swimming pool was later named after him.

☆ **JOHN CORNFORTH**. He won the Nobel Prize for chemistry in 1975 for his research on 'the stereochemistry of enzyme-catalysed reactins'.

☆ **KAY COTTEE**. In 1988, she was the first woman to sail solo non-stop around the world.

☆ **MILO DUNPHY**. Trained as an architect in the 1950s, he set up the Total Environment Centre in Sydney and devoted his energies to preserving wilderness areas against mining, woodchipping and development, until his death in 1996. We have his lobbying of politicians to thank for much of the national park space in NSW.

☆ **BERNARD 'MIDGET' FARRELLY**. Born in Dee Why, he won the world's first official surfboard riding championships, held at Manly in 1964, and kept winning Australian titles.

☆ **JEFF FENECH**. Born in Marrickville, he won world boxing titles in three categories: bantamweight (1985), superbantamweight (1987) and featherweight (1988). He's best remembered for telling his fans 'I love youse all'.

☆ **DAWN FRASER**. The world's greatest swimmer, she won gold medals for the 100 metres freestyle at the 1956, 1960 and 1964 Olympics but was barred from the next Olympics by the Australian Swimming Union, allegedly for rebellious behaviour. In 1988, she was elected to NSW parliament as the independent member for Balmain, where she used to run a pub and where the local swimming pool is named after her. She was voted out in 1991.

☆ **MARY GAUDRON**. A lawyer active on social justice issues, she was appointed the youngest-ever Federal Court judge in 1974 (aged 31), then was NSW Solicitor-General from 1981 to 1987, when she became the first woman appointed to the High Court.

☆ **FRED HOLLOWS**. Although he was born in New Zealand and did most of his sight-saving work in central Australia, Africa and Asia, Sydney claims Dr Hollows. Trained as an ophthalmologist, he founded the first Aboriginal Medical Centre in Redfern in 1971 and developed anti-blindness programs around the world. He died in 1995.

☆ **IAN KIERNAN**. A restorer of historic houses and a long-distance yachty, he organised a mass clean-up of Sydney Harbour in 1989, which produced tonnes of rubbish and raised public consciousness about pollution. It grew into the annual Clean Up Australia Day.

☆ **JACK MUNDEY**. As leader of the Builders' Labourers Federation in the early 1970s, Mundey persuaded other unionists to refuse to work on projects that could damage Sydney's heritage or environment. We have his 'green bans' to thank for the preservation of numerous buildings and natural areas. He was later elected to Sydney City Council and chaired its planning committee in the mid 1980s.

☆ **TED NOFFS**. A Methodist minister, he set up the Wayside Chapel in Kings Cross in 1964, turning it into Australia's first drug referral centre, and then founded a series of Life Education Centres to prevent, as well as treat, drug addiction.

☆ **ANDREW OLLE**. An ABC radio broadcaster and TV journalist acclaimed for his interviewing style and his fairness, he died of a brain tumour in 1995.

☆ **PAT O'SHANE**. In 1976, Patricia O'Shane became the first Aboriginal woman to be admitted to the bar in Australia. In 1981, she became the first woman to head a government department when she was appointed to run the NSW Department of Aboriginal Affairs. In 1986, she became the first Aboriginal to be appointed a magistrate.

☆ **ANNE SARGEANT**. Australia's greatest netball player, she played in Australia's world-beating teams in 1979 and 1983, and captained Australia between 1983 and 1987.

☆ **DICK SMITH**. He used the profits from a chain of electrical stores to do charitable works, go on adventurous journeys (including the first solo round-the-world helicopter flight in 1983), and to start the successful *Australian Geographic* magazine.

36
eating

*m*odern Australian cuisine, as pioneered in Sydney, is a unique style that blends Italian generosity, French finesse, Asian spicing and the good old Aussie barbecue. Sydney eaters (and chefs) are faddy, so this month's hot zone can be next month's cold storage. But as we went to press, these were the best places to experience the new Sydney cooking:

☆ **BREAKFAST.** Bills, 433 Liverpool Street, Darlinghurst (9360 9631). Bill tosses a fine ricotta hot cake, with superior orange juice and coffee. It's cheap. On weekends, Sydney's most lavish morning spread appears at The Bathers Pavilion, 4 The Esplanade, Balmoral (9968 1133). It's almost expensive.

☆ **BUSH FOOD.** Edna's Table, MLC Centre, Martin Place (9231 1400). If the Count of La Perouse had got to Botany Bay first, this is how we'd have been using local ingredients such as

kangaroo and emu for the past 200 years.
It's almost expensive.

☆ **BUSINESS LUNCH.** CBD, upstairs at 75 York
Street in the city (9299 8911). Almost expensive.

☆ **BUZZ.** Bayswater Brasserie, 32 Bayswater
Road, Kings Cross (9357 2177). It offers
innovative food, medium prices and the chance
to spot Nicole Kidman and Sam Neill.

☆ **CHINESE.** Or neo-Chinese, really. Wockpool,
under the Imax cinema, Darling Harbour
(9211 9888). Medium-priced.

☆ **DESIGN.** With fine food as well: Rockpool,
107 George Street, the Rocks (9252 1888), a
symphony in stainless steel. Darley Street Thai,
28 Bayswater Road, Kings Cross (9358 6530),
like eating inside a watermelon. Bennelong,
Sydney Opera House (9250 7548), Joern Utzon
provided the structure, the artichoke lamps add
the drama. All expensive.

☆ **FISH AND CHIPS.** The Bottom of the
Harbour, 21 The Esplanade, Balmoral
(9969 7911). Medium-priced.

☆ **FRENCH.** Claude's, 10 Oxford Street,
Woollahra (9331 2325). Or if you want to
include a two-hour train ride: Cleopatra,
118 Cleopatra Street, Blackheath
(047 87 8456). Both expensive.

☆ **GREEK.** The Hellenic Club, top floor of
251 Elizabeth Street in the city (9261 4910).
It's stodgy but satisfying and cheap, with a

view of Hyde Park and good retsina.

☆ **HAMBURGERS.** Burgerman, 249 Bondi Road, Bondi (9130 4888) or Charlie's Cafe, 7–41 Cowper Wharf Roadway, Woolloomooloo (9358 4443). Cheap.

☆ **IMAGINATION.** Tetsuya's, 729 Darling Street, Rozelle (9555 1017). Attempts to see French and Japanese influences in the cooking of Tetsuya Wakuda miss the point—these creations come from individual passion. Expensive but wonderful.

☆ **ITALIAN.** The battle for best is between Buon Ricordo, 108 Boundary Street, Paddington (9360 6729) and Lucio's, 47 Windsor Street, Paddington (9380 5996). Buon Ricordo's food is more adventurous and Lucio's atmosphere is more relaxing. Both are almost expensive.

☆ **JAPANESE.** Matsukaze, level 1 of 2 Chifley Square in the city (9229 0191). Medium-priced.

☆ **MIDNIGHT.** The Golden Century, 393 Sussex Street, Chinatown. (9212 3901). Cheap.

☆ **SLEAZE.** The Bourbon and Beefsteak, 24 Darlinghurst Road, Kings Cross (9358 1144). It offers Las Vegas atmosphere 24 hours a day, and the guys at the next table might be plotting a murder. Medium-priced.

☆ **PIZZA.** The Pig and the Olive, 71a Macleay Street, Potts Point (9357 3745). Offers trendy toppings like duck that would offend traditionalists, but the flavour's all there. Cheap.

☆ **SUSHI.** The sushi bar in the Sydney Fish
   Markets, Blackwattle Bay, Pyrmont
   (9552 2872). Medium-priced.

☆ **TAPAS.** Casa Asturiana, 77 Liverpool Street in
   the city (9264 1010). Cheap.

☆ **THAI.** Sailors Thai, 106 George Street, the
   Rocks (9251 2466). Medium-priced.

☆ **TRADITION.** Beppi's, Cnr Stanley and Yurong
   Streets, East Sydney (9360 4558). Since 1956,
   Beppi Polese has been the patriarch of smooth
   service and Italian integrity.

☆ **VEGETARIAN.** Red Kite, corner of Roscoe
   and Gould Streets, Bondi (9365 0432).
   Medium-priced.

☆ **VIETNAMESE.** Minh, 510 Marrickville Road,
   Dulwich Hill (9560 0465) or Thanh Binh, 111
   King Street, Newtown (9727 9729). Both cheap.

☆ **VIEW.** With fine food: The Bathers Pavilion,
   4 The Esplanade, Balmoral Beach (9968 1133),
   sand and ocean. The Boathouse on Blackwattle
   Bay, end of Ferry Road, Glebe (9518 9011),
   the skyline from below. Forty One, top floor of
   2 Chifley Square in the city (9221 2500), the
   skyline from above. All are almost-expensive.

☆ **YUM CHA.** The Silver Spring, upstairs at
   191 Hay Street, Haymarket (9211 2232) or
   The Dragon, 455 Victoria Avenue, Chatswood
   (9415 2785). Both cheap.

37
food stores

S ydney has become so obsessed with eating in the past decade that the suburbs now overflow with providores, of which these are some personal favourites ...

☆ **A C BUTCHERY,** 174 Marion Street, Leichhardt, supplies the best restaurants with specialist meats, great sausages, prosciutto, etc.

☆ **ACCOUTREMENT,** 611 Military Road, Mosman, has a huge range of kitchen equipment and arranges cooking lessons from chefs.

☆ **B AND J LIZARD,** 186 Harris Street, Ultimo, is tops for fruit and veg and jams.

☆ **THE BAY TREE,** 40 Holdsworth Street, Woollahra, is a smaller, quainter version of Accoutrement.

☆ **THE CHEESE SHOP,** 797 Military Road, Mosman is run by fanatics for fanatics.

☆ **DEMETER BAKERY,** 65 Derwent Street, Glebe, has dense chunky bread that's too tasty to be as healthy as they claim.

☆ **THE ESSENTIAL INGREDIENT,** 4 Australia Street, Camperdown, has cookbooks, equipment and quality ingredients.

☆ **FIVE STAR GOURMET,** 13 Willoughby

Road, Crows Nest, is a deli/supermarket with endless variety.

☆ **NORTON STREET MARKET,** 55 Norton Street, Leichhardt, has all the Italian esoterica in season, at bargain prices.

☆ **THE PRINCE CENTRE,** 8 Quay Street, Haymarket, has ingredients for any Asian recipe, including Chinese, Thai and Vietnamese.

☆ **RUSSELL'S NATURAL FOOD MARKETS,** 55 Glebe Point Road, Glebe, has deli bits, fruit, veg and stuff for allergy sufferers.

☆ **SIMMONE LOGUE,** at either 349 Darling Street, Balmain or 479 Oxford Street, Paddington, does gorgeous cakes.

☆ **SWEET ART,** 96 Oxford Street, Paddington, will hand-decorate cakes to any pattern.

☆ **SWEET WILLIAM CHOCOLATES,** 4 William Street, Paddington, is a quaint little shop offering coffee, tea or indulgences.

☆ **SIMON JOHNSON QUALITY FOODS,** 181 Harris Street, Pyrmont, is the trendsetter for both chefs and home cooks with great Australian cheeses and breads, and imports of olive oil, teas and other wonders.

☆ **TOKYO MART,** shop 27, Northbridge Plaza, Sailors Bay Rd, has all things Japanese.

And then, of course, there's the **Sydney Fish Markets** at Blackwattle Bay, where shopkeepers and chefs bid for the best off the boats before breakfast, and you pay more for less later in the day.

38
coffee

*t*echnically, Sydney's best coffee is not quite in Sydney. To get it, you must travel west from the town centre for two hours by train (or car, if you insist). The journey will be no hardship, since the train glides spectacularly upwards into the Blue Mountains. And when you've tumbled out at Blackheath station and wandered down Govett's Leap Road to Vulcan's Cafe, you'll reach not only the most luscious espresso you've ever sipped, but the best cooking in the mountains. And you'll be on the brink of superb bushland to walk off the caffeine.

During the 1980s, Philip Searle and Barry Ross ran one of Sydney's poshest restaurants, Oasis Seros, but in the 1990s they became disillusioned with the fickleness of Sydney foodies and headed for the hills. They found an old bakery at Blackheath and started using the wood-fired oven to roast meats, fish and vegetables, and to bake perfect puddings. It's called Vulcan's after the Roman god of fire.

They also spent months researching beans, blends and roasting methods until they achieved their idea of heaven in a cup. They keep the details of the coffee a close secret, but they'll let you drink it from breakfast till supper on Fridays, Saturdays and Sundays. The rest of the week Phillip does paintings and Barry does gardening—along with consuming their own coffee, of course.

But perhaps when you saw this chapter's title you were envisaging more of a scene—not just the cup but the whole coffee culture: tiny tables crammed with black-clad people gossiping about the latest movies they've made. As a matter of fact, Vulcan's has a fair bit of that sort of atmosphere but if you'd rather not be so far from the inner city, you can look for these:

☆ **BAR COLUZZI**, 322 Victoria Street, Darlinghurst. An institution since 1957, it's so cramped inside that most customers prefer to sit on tiny plastic stools on the footpath and trip the world as it passes by. The racing crowd also goes there before early morning training at Randwick Racecourse.

☆ **TROPICANA**, 227 Victoria Street, Darlinghurst. The furniture is stained, the cakes are sometimes just short of fresh, but the toasted snacks are cheap and the scene is sizzling. So many budding filmmakers meet here that they've started an annual festival of short films. Here's where the junkies come when they get the munchies at 5am (not so much ambience as ambulance).

☆ **RUSHCUTTERS BAY KIOSK,** in the park off New Beach Road, Rushcutters Bay. It was once a toilet block but that's no longer evident. Surrounded by trees, boats and cricketing children, you'll feel positively wholesome as you order your second latte.

☆ **DOV,** corner of Forbes and Burton Streets, Darlinghurst. It's across the road from an art college so the chaotic service is as important as good coffee and late hours.

☆ **NOSTIMO,** 113 Queen Street, Woollahra. It offers not just the usual espresso variations but sweet sludgy Greek coffee as well, plus Greco-Roman snacks.

☆ **THE OLD SYDNEY COFFEE SHOP,** ground floor of the Strand Arcade in the city. This is as much historical curio as caffeine fix, serving teas, coffees and hot chocolates since 1891.

Coffee has become so much a part of the Sydney culture that great cafes can be found just about anywhere. There's plenty of steam in these:

☆ **SEJUICED,** 472 Bronte Road, Bronte. A sidewalk scene in summer and winter, across the road from a beach with a powerful undertow.

☆ **BAR ITALIA,** 169 Norton Street, Leichhardt. This is where the old Italians and the new trendies meet for coffee, cake, gelato and cheap basic pasta.

☆ **THE OLD FISH SHOP,** corner of King and Church Streets, Newtown. It's in your face and onto the street until midnight.

☆ **GLEBE COFFEE ROASTER,** inside the Forest Lodge Hotel, 117 Arundel Street, Glebe. They roast their own beans on the spot, then let you choose your own mix of strengths and nationalities.

If you're new to Sydney's coffee culture, you must learn its language. An *espresso* (strong and black in a small cup) is also known as a short black. A *long black* is in a bigger cup with more water, so it is not as strong as a double espresso. *Caffe latte* is an espresso with hot milk. It is often served in a glass which burns your fingers when you pick it up. A *flat white* is a milky latte in a cup. A *macchiato* is a short black with a splash of milk. A *cappuccino* is an espresso in a big cup topped with thick milk froth and

chocolate powder. A *skinny cap* is a cino with skim milk. And a *babycino* is milk froth with chocolate powder, designed to allow children or people with caffeine sensitivities to enjoy the scene without the sleeplessness.

39
wine

a ustralia's first wine was produced in 1795 at the Parramatta farm of a German free settler named Phillip Schaffer, who made 90 gallons of something he called 'Rhinewine'. It worked well enough to start a fad.

But, 'the Father of the Australian wine industry' was a Scot named James Busby, who arrived in Sydney in the late 1820s with a lot of vine cuttings he'd collected in France. He donated some to the Botanic Gardens so other farmers could use them, and he started a vineyard in the Hunter River valley, about 200 km north of Sydney. He called his farm Kirkton. From it grew Australia's first viticulture region—the Hunter Valley.

Busby was followed to the Hunter in 1840 by Henry Lindeman, a doctor who spent as much time promoting the health properties of wine (compared with the 'moral and physical degeneration' of spirits) as he did growing grapes at his property, called Cawarra. He found that the white grape that worked best was verdelho and the best red grapes were shiraz and cabernet sauvignon.

These days, Sydney people are big wine drinkers—we consume 19 litres each a year (compared with a national average of 18) of which 42 per cent is white, 36 per cent is red and 32 per cent is sparkling. But we don't feel any particular dedication to the Hunter, even though it's a popular spot for weekend tasting tours. We're just as likely to drink wines from the more adventurous Margaret River region of Western Australia, or the more reliable Barossa region of South Australia.

If Sydneysiders did choose to be patriotic (or do I mean urbiotic?) to their local drops—that is, to wines grown within half a day's drive from the city—they now have a huge array from which to choose. In the past 20 years, new grape regions have been appearing up and down the state, just west of the Great Dividing Range of mountains. The boom area is a strip directly west of Sydney from Mudgee down to Young via Orange and Cowra.

These are some interesting local wines:

☆ Mudgee—Rosemount Estate Mountain Blue shiraz cabernet; Andrew Harris shiraz cabernet or Reserve cabernet sauvignon.

☆ Cowra—Hungerford Hill Young Cowra cabernet sauvignon; McWilliams Barwang shiraz.

☆ Orange—Reynolds Orange chardonnay; Canobolas-Smith chardonnay; Canobolas-Smith Alchemy (merlot, shiraz, cabernet).

☆ the Hastings Valley—Cassegrain Chambourcin.

☆ the Hunter—McWilliams Mount Pleasant Elizabeth semillon; Brokenwood Cricket Pitch

116

semillon/sauvignon blanc; Pepper Tree semillon/sauvignon blanc; Tyrell's Stevens shiraz.

☆ Griffith (way south)—Cranswick Estate unoaked chardonnay or semillon or shiraz; De Bortoli Noble One (botrytis semillon); and West End Three Bridges botrytis semillon.

The best **wine shops** from which to sample these sorts of local drops would include The Ultimo Wine Centre, 460 Jones Street, Ultimo; Vintage Cellars, 396 New South Head Road, Double Bay; and Camperdown Cellars, 21 Kingston Road, Camperdown.

Most good Sydney **restaurants** keep a few locals in their cellars, but the most patriotic is Mario's in East Sydney, which offers only wines made either in NSW or in Italy. Other interesting wine lists with a NSW emphasis can be found at Cicada in Kings Cross, Rockpool in the Rocks, The Bathers Pavilion at Balmoral, Forty One in the city, and Darling Mills in Glebe. One Hunter Valley wine has a special place in Sydneysiders' hearts. In 1982, when the Labor premier Neville Wran was at the peak of his popularity, he was under pressure to move to the national political stage and help his Labor colleagues in Canberra. He held a media conference to announce that he was going to stay in Sydney. Asked how he had reached this decision, Wran said: 'At 11 o'clock last night, halfway through a bottle of Rosemount Gold Medal chardonnay'. That wine has been a bestseller ever since.

40
pubs

*t*he Sydney pub is not what it was, thank God. Now that wine and coffee have replaced beer as the national beverages, pubs have been forced to adapt or close. They've installed espresso machines and they've rented out their old dining rooms to trendy chefs. Some have even started serving beer that doesn't taste like it's already been round once.

A few of the town's most interesting pubs are:

☆ **THE FRIEND IN HAND,** 58 Cowper Street, Glebe. It so trad it's weird, but with Italian food and crab racing on Wednesday nights.

☆ **THE GREENWOOD,** Greenwood Plaza, 36 Blue Street, North Sydney. In an old sandstone schoolhouse, it's a hangout for what were once called yuppies, but there's a courtyard with plenty of space to escape the creepiest.

☆ **THE HAROLD PARK,** 115 Wigram Road, Glebe, which has rooms devoted to standup comedy, literary readings, political debates, and a form of country dancing called bootscooting.

☆ **THE LONDON,** 234 Darling Street, Balmain. Its verandah is the viewing platform from which the Balmain literati watch the traffic go by.

☆ **THE LORD DUDLEY,** 236 Jersey Road,

Woollahra. So covered with foliage and so filled with old wood, it almost succeeds in looking like an English village retreat.

☆ **THE LORD NELSON,** corner of Kent and Argyle Streets, the Rocks. Built out of sandstone about 1840, and staunchly maintaining a British naval atmosphere, it now brews its own 'boutique' beers.

☆ **THE OAKS,** 118 Military Road, Neutral Bay. It's a sprawling mansion with a huge beer garden and rooms to meet a range of tastes.

☆ **THE WOOLLAHRA HOTEL,** corner of Queen and Moncur Streets, Woollahra. This is where well-dressed youngsters pick each other up while listening to a jazz band and waiting for a table in the adjoining Bistro Moncur. There's also a back bar where a few old lags sip over their racing forms.

41
bars

a bar is different, of course, from a pub—it will usually have a wider range of cocktails and a narrower range of beers. And, in Sydney, it needs to have either a view or a 'scene' to justify its existence. Here's a sampling of meeting places near the city centre:

☆ **BARONS,** 5 Roslyn Street, Kings Cross, a late-night institution where you can still get a drink and an argument after midnight.

☆ **THE BAYSWATER BRASSERIE,** 32 Bayswater Road, Kings Cross, offers cocktail craziness for young trendies, some of whom are not even waiting for a table in the attached restaurant.

☆ **THE BONDI ICEBERGS CLUB,** on Notts Avenue at the southern end of Bondi Beach, has cheap beer, no serious dress rules and a great view.

☆ **THE GEORGE STREET BAR,** in the Regent Hotel, 199 George St in the city, has pizzas and the prospect of being chatted up by a wealthier class of suit.

☆ **THE HORIZONS BAR,** on the 36th floor of the ANA hotel, 176 Cumberland Street, the

Rocks, has high prices but you're paying for leather armchairs and a panoramic view.

☆ **THE MARBLE BAR,** under the Hilton Hotel on George Street in the city, is a piece of Sydney preserved from the Beaux Arts era, with marble, stained glass, paintings, mirrors and jazz on Fridays and Saturdays.

☆ **THE RITZ CARLTON HOTEL,** 93 Macquarie Street in the city, has a clubby, wintry sort of bar serving fine martinis in what used to be a VD clinic.

☆ **THE ROOF TOP BAR,** up a lot of steps at the Kings Cross Hotel, 248 William Street, Kings Cross, is a bloodhouse on Saturday nights, favoured by New Zealand tourists, but it has a garden and a view of the city.

☆ **THE SPORTS BARD,** 32 Campbell Parade, Bondi Beach, is really a casual eating place, where the noisy crowd lingers over drinks, tasty food and pool tables until 11pm. The word 'bard' is not a misprint—it's the by-product of the State's strange licensing laws.

☆ **THE TAXI CLUB,** 42 Flinders Street, Darlinghurst, is for insomniac alcoholics with a taste for the low life. It's open till 6am.

☆ **THE TOP OF THE TOWN,** on top of 227 Victoria Street, Kings Cross, has a fine view and 1970s decor, hence it's known as 'the bar that time forgot'.

42
hotels

S ydney had inns from the 1790s but the first grand hotel seems to have been Petty's, built in 1834 at Wynyard Square. A suite cost 10 shillings a night and included a bathroom but not running water, which was brought by a maid. An ad in the 1850s said Petty's 'surpassed all other accommodation in comfort, privacy, convenience and healthy situation'.

Sydney grew slowly from there. In 1965, there were just four top class hotels: The Australia, the Chevron Hilton, the Carlton Rex, and the Wentworth. It was recorded at the time that Sydney had 350 air-conditioned rooms with their own bathrooms. Then the world suddenly decided we were worth visiting. Now there are 5000 hotel rooms classified as 'top class'. The grandest establishments, worth a visit by locals purely for stickybeaking, are:

☆ **THE INTERCONTINENTAL,** 117 Macquarie Street in the city. It's inserted within the sandstone Treasury Building from 1851 (which was itself built on the site of Governor Phillip's first grape plantation in 1791), so it has a lovely palm court with internal balconies.

Afternoon tea with a string quartet is a weekend treat.

☆ **THE OBSERVATORY,** 89 Kent Street, Millers Point. Built in the early 1990s to look like an early 1890s mansion, it's small and elegant and contains an interesting Italian restaurant called Galileo.

☆ **THE PARK HYATT,** 7 Hickson Road, Circular Quay. It wraps around the western end of the Quay, just under the Bridge, and looks across to the Opera House.

☆ **THE REGENT,** 199 George Street in the city. It was the first extravagant hotel of the 1980s, so of course it has an overpowering atrium loaded with polished marble. Its chef, Serge Dansereau, pioneered the use of unusual Australian ingredients in the Kables restaurant.

☆ **THE SEBEL TOWN HOUSE,** 23 Elizabeth Bay Road, Kings Cross. Founded in the early 1960s, it rapidly became the Sydney home for visiting rock stars and actors. By today's standards, it's fairly grotty for a grand hotel but the attraction for the stars is its discretion—they can do *anything they like* in their rooms.

☆ **THE SHERATON ON THE PARK,** 161 Elizabeth Street in the city. With soaring columns and a serious staircase, it mimics the lavishness of Parisian grand hotels and does a fine arvo tea.

Hip trippers of modest means tend to go for **L'otel**, 114 Darlinghurst Road, Darlinghurst, and can reasonably expect to be squeezed next to a model or a rock singer at the bar. People seeking beach views from their rooms head for **Ravesi's Guest House** at Bondi. And seekers of the perfect dirty weekend can't go further than **Jonah's** at Whale Beach in the city's far north, which offers fine views and fine food when you get tired of other activities.

43
bookshops

*f*or those who want to read mainstream bestsellers, there are many Dymocks and Angus &
Robertson stores scattered through city and
suburbs. But for more specialised tastes, and for
stimulating browsing, here are some of my favourite
wordmarkets.

☆ **ABBEY'S,** 131 York Street in the city. Not too
strong on display, but superb in crime fiction,
reference books, foreign language and
university texts.

☆ **THE ABC SHOPS.** There's a big one midtown
in the Queen Victoria Building and several
others in the suburbs, and they sell books,
videos, records and toys that are supposed to
have connections with ABC radio or TV
programs. That turns out to mean comedy,
travel, history, politics and Bananas in Pyjamas.

☆ **ARIEL,** 42 Oxford Street, Paddington. It does a
nice line in art, detective fiction, popular
culture, sociology, travel and food, and, best of
all, it's open till midnight every day.

☆ **BERKELOUW,** 19 Oxford Street, Paddington,
opposite Ariel. Some new books downstairs but
a great array of second-hand stuff upstairs,

particularly Australiana, and a comfortable cafe.

☆ **THE CONSTANT READER,** 27 Willoughby Road, Crows Nest. Like any good bookshop, it reflects the eccentricities of its owner. Peter Kirby lists the specialties of his store as 'Australiana, graphic arts, computers, travel—both guides and vicarious—children's books, plus the usual sex and violence'.

☆ **GLEEBOOKS,** 49 Glebe Point Road, Glebe. It nominates its specialties as the humanities and Australian and international literature, but it's also strong on popular culture and science fiction. Its branch at 191 Glebe Point Road has second-hand and kids' books.

☆ **GOULD'S,** 32 King Street, Newtown. For bookoholics without dust allergies, there are thousands of square metres of second-hand treasures here, though Gould's will never win prizes for filing.

☆ **LESLEY MACKAY'S,** 346 New South Head Road, Double Bay. It's useful for literary classics, gardening, design, history and the latest arty fiction. There's a cramped but lively children's department just across the road.

☆ **NICHOLAS POUNDER,** 346 New South Head Road, Double Bay. Here's the town's top finder of rare books and first editions.

44
fashion

Sydney has become Australia's fashion capital in recent years, with new designers leaping from here to the world. Hillary Clinton wears Helen Kaminski's hats, Madonna wears Morrissey Edmiston, and Nicole Kidman wears Collette Dinnigan. So how can Sydneysiders get hold of this sort of stuff for themselves?

Although Mosman and Chatswood have their fair share of boutiques, the eastern suburbs is the main direction for ready-to-wear designer clothes—from Crown Street, Surry Hills (the suburb that is the centre of clothing manufacture of all kinds) along Oxford Street, Paddington to Queen Street, Woollahra, with more conservative shopping in Double Bay.

Hip style-stalkers go to Crown Street, notably to the very rock-n-roll Wheels & Doll Baby or to Pepa Mejia, which represents around two dozen independent Australian designers.

Headline-grabbing lingerie and frock maker Collette Dinnigan is located in William Street, a tiny offshoot of Oxford Street. Jodie Boffa's classic dresses and suits can be found at 26 Glenmore Road. Award-winning Zimmerman is near where Oxford and Queen Streets meet in Woollahra, Lisa

Ho's emporium of style is right on the corner, and Akira Isogawa, who marries occidental stylings with oriental materials, is a few doors down at 12a Queen Street.

Original local and overseas labels can be found in a myriad of suave stores along Oxford Street itself, such as Zambesi, Bracewell and Robby Ingham (separate stores for men and women) and Marc's (which is mainly male). Snappy Australian-designed separates, suits and evening wear (for women only) in a range of prices and style-consciousness can be sought at Scanlan & Theodore, Von Troska and Black Vanity—the latter two, like so many other designers, also have outlets in the CBD, particularly in the boutique-stacked Strand Arcade and QVB. Spunky local celebrity designers Morrissey Edmiston can be found in shop 63 of the Strand.

The MLC Centre, between King Street and Martin Place, and the more recent addition, Sky-garden, from Castlereagh Street to the Pitt Street Mall, are also loaded with prestige shopping opportunities.

European couture is slung along a style corridor in Castlereagh Street and around the intersection of King Street. Chanel, Gucci, Louis Vuitton, Yves St Laurent, Hermes, Moschino and Dior rub tailored shoulders. Max Mara and Nina Ricci are on Chifley Plaza, Georgio Armani is on Market Street with his Emporio in Martin Place, and Gianni Versace is around the corner on Elizabeth Street. (The main city store for Sydney's doyenne of fashion, Carla Zampatti, is down the road at 143 Elizabeth.)

Serious Australian jewellers also cluster on the Castlereagh strip: all-purpose Hardy Brothers, Paspaley Pearls, and Percy Marks, for pearls and opals. New York's Tiffany & Co is a gemstone's throw away on Chifley Plaza. Bulgari is on Market Street, opposite David Jones department store.

Three notable local jewellers are in the Strand Arcade: Rox, contemporary rings and things using precious stones; Love & Hatred, affordable wit in precious metals; and Dinosaur Designs, locally-made resin objects to decorate both the body and the home (there are also branches in the Rocks and on Oxford Street, Paddington). Victoria Spring, maker of romantic costume jewellery, is in William Street, off Oxford.

For the cheerful straw hats that Hillary hoorayed, head for Helen Kaminski's shop within the Argyle Department Store at the Rocks. The more adventurous may prefer Isabelle Klompe, 19 Evans Street, Bronte while men seeking the bush look can find their Akubras at Strand Hatters in the Strand Arcade.

For the other end of the body, Donna May Bollinger at 379 South Dowling Street, Darlinghurst creates exquisite hand-made shoes, and men and women who want to be part of an Australian legend put their toes into R M Williams riding boots at 389 George Street in the city.

45
antiques

Sydneysiders like to take Sunday drives to the Blue Mountains or the southern town of Berrima to search for bargains in antiques. The bargain theory is another urban myth.

Queen Street, Woollahra, is the place for the serious collector. Among the 20 or so purveyors between Oxford and Moncur Streets are Copeland & De Soos, with arts both deco and nouveau; Antiques de France, with decorative country objects; Anne Schofield's jewellery and ornaments; Michael Greene's silverware and glassware; Re-entombed Galleries' ancient sculptures; Charles Hewitt's frames and prints; and Tim McCormick's Australiana.

Further towards Bondi Junction on Oxford Street is the Woollahra Antiques Centre, a warehouse filled with individual sellers of bric-a-brac or there's the Sydney Antiques Centre on South Dowling Street, Surry Hills, en route to the airport.

For cheaper old furniture the strip of Parramatta Road near Johnston Street, Annandale, and the Enmore end of King Street, Newtown contain shops selling more than junk. For ultra modern furniture, try Flinders Street, Darlinghurst, with Space at 111 and the Design Warehouse at 67.

46
galleries

*t*he Art Gallery of NSW was founded in 1885 and remains, in ever expanding form, at the edge of a park called The Domain, just east of the CBD. It rewards the expenditure of a wet afternoon and its Yiribana Gallery on the lower ground floor is a helpful introduction to Aboriginal art. But if you insist on owning rather than just looking, a wander through the Victorian village of Paddington offers an alarming range of opportunities.

☆ The Sherman Galleries, at the corner of Cascade and Hargrave Streets, and on Goodhope Street, exhibit contemporary painters and sculptors.

☆ Roslyn Oxley Gallery, Soudan Lane (off Hampden Street), displays big-name cutting-edge artists.

☆ Josef Lebovic, on the corner of Cascade and Paddington Streets, has an outstanding collection of original Australian and international prints, photographs and works on paper.

☆ Rex Irwin Art Dealer, above 38 Queen Street, Woollahra, represents some of Australia's

biggest names as well as the internationally
famous.

☆ Byron Mapp Gallery, 178 Oxford Street, shows
some of the country's most celebrated
photographers.

☆ Authentic Aboriginal art is found at Hogarth
Galleries/Aboriginal Arts Centre, 7 Walker
Lane, Paddington.

In neighbouring Surry Hills, the emphasis at Ray
Hughes Gallery, 270 Devonshire Street, is on
vibrant Australian work. In the CBD, these are
worth a visit: Mori Gallery, 168 Day Street,
showing established and unknown contemporary
Australian artists; Gallery 4A, 3rd floor, 405 Sussex
Street, Haymarket, with experimental Asian and
Australian stuff; Yuill/Crowley, 8th floor, the Block,
428 George Street, with avant garde modernism;
Quadrivium, level 2, Queen Victoria Building, with
Aboriginal and Asian art, designer objects, and
sculpture.

Further west, the Annandale Galleries, 110 Tra-
falgar Street, Annandale, represent a wide range of
living local painters and sculptors and offer graphic
exhibitions by older masters; and Utopia Art,
50 Parramatta Road, Stanmore, specialises in Aboriginal work, especially that of Emily Kngwarreye
(the most famous recent Aboriginal painter).

47
shopping

Sydney's first big store was started in 1838 by a Welsh immigrant named David Jones. It was a drapery 'in commodious premises opposite the general post office'. As it grew, it spawned competitors.

John Gowing arrived in 1857 at the age of 21 and went to work for David Jones; when he felt he'd learned enough, he opened his own department store in 1868. It soon became an important supplier of practical clothing and accessories for country men on their regular trips to the city, giving rise to the catchphrase 'gone to Gowings'.

Two brothers named Joseph and Albert Grace arrived in the early 1880s, sold drapery door to door and opened their first shop in George Street near Central Railway in 1885. Albert lived long enough to realise that Sydney was going to be a city of suburbs, and opened branches at Bondi and Parramatta in 1933.

Meanwhile, an entrepreneur named Harold Christmas saw an opportunity to undercut these elegant emporia and opened a bargain basement store in Pitt Street in 1924. Instead of naming it after himself (a lost opportunity, if you ask me) he named it after an American cut-price chain called Woolworth.

These four proved to have the staying power. While the other legendary names in Sydney's mercantile history—Farmer's, Mark Foys, Marcus Clark's and Anthony Horderns—faded away, the big four keep growing. David Jones is our most upmarket department store, with two centres in the CBD and nine suburban sites. Grace Brothers, with 15 stores in the city and suburbs, is now controlled by Melbourne's Coles-Myer. Gowings, with a main store on Market Street and branches in George Street and Oxford Street, is still the no-nonsense clothes and equipment shop for boys and men and for women who want to look like them, and continues to produce a mail-order catalogue for its customers. Woolworth's is everywhere, employing 95 000 people across Australia.

There is also a glittering array of stores housed in the Queen Victoria Building, occupying a block on George Street opposite the Town Hall. Dating from 1898, it was built on the site of an old market and refurbished to 19th century elegance in 1986 at a cost of $75 million.

Running from George Street to the Pitt Street Mall and dating from 1892, the Strand Arcade is stacked with quality stores and smart boutiques. Along with the Argyle Department Store in the Rocks, these are pleasant places to shop if you don't require bargains.

Alternatively, you can go hunting through one of Sydney's weekly markets. The best is held in the grounds of Paddington Public School, Oxford Street, every Saturday. Paddington Bazaar is where young designers, jewellers and potters try out their latest creations, while buskers try out their latest songs. Something more like the traditional flea market is held in the grounds of Balmain Congregational Church (corner of Darling Street and Curtis Road) every Saturday. And Sydney's ferals (a youth cult somewhere between punks and hippies) prefer the Saturday market in the grounds of Glebe Public School on Glebe Point Road.

At the beginning of George Street each Saturday and Sunday, there's the Rocks Market, touristy but useful for arty crafty ornaments, leather, jewellery and toys. Paddy's Market, on the corner of Hay and Thomas Streets, Haymarket, on Saturdays and Sundays, has everyday household stuff, clothes, flowers, CDs and gadgets.

And all Sydney residents, at least once in their lives, need to get up early and have a look at the hectares of food and flowers at Flemington Produce Markets, off Parramatta Road in Flemington. This is where just about everything we eat gets into the hands of our shopkeepers or restaurateurs.

48
loos

i t's a relief to learn that finding relief is not difficult in Sydney. If there's no public toilet nearby, you can pop into a pub or cinema without needing to buy a drink or see a movie. But it's harder to find a loo with character, where you can marvel at the creativity of the designer after you've removed the urgency from your visit. Here's my theory on the city's most interesting toilets.

☆ **THE UPPER FLOOR OF RESTAURANT 41,** in the Chifley Tower, corner of Hunter and Elizabeth Streets. You'll need to be a customer of the restaurant to experience this, which is no hardship since the food is excellent. On top of one of our tallest skyscrapers, this is the loo with the view—the most spectacular in Sydney, maybe the world, through wrap-around glass windows. They even provide chairs so you can stare for as long as you like.

☆ **GROUND FLOOR OF THE STATE THEATRE,** 49 Market Street. In keeping with the gothic absurdity of the whole cinema, built in 1929, the loos are vast, with gilded statues, velvet curtains and ceiling paintings. The ladies is The Butterfly Room.

☆ **LEVEL I OF THE QUEEN VICTORIA BUILDING,** corner of Market and George Streets. The whole structure is a beautiful restoration of what was called an 'American Romanesque' design in 1898, and the loos carry through the theme with multicoloured glass, tiles and polished woodwork.

☆ **GROUND FLOOR OF THE OBSERVATORY HOTEL,** 89 Kent Street, Millers Point. The loos themselves are elegantly efficient, with tiles and dark polished wood, but the anterooms are a delight, offering international newspapers, shoe cleaning equipment and toiletries.

☆ **IN BUON RICORDO RESTAURANT,** 108 Boundary Street, Paddington. Full-length, three-dimensional paintings on the doors clearly define which gender is intended to pass through.

☆ **IN BILSON'S RESTAURANT,** Overseas Passenger Terminal, Circular Quay West. The designer, George Freedman, decided to match the theme to the user, so the men's has a vertical towel cupboard thrusting up from testicular washbasins on either side, while the women's has white ceramic basins in the shape of eggs. The walls are covered in glass mosaic tiles (turquoise for women, azure for men), the doors are walnut veneer, and white marble divides the cubicles. If only more builders of Sydney properties gave lavatorial design such a priority.

49
sport

*f*or all our reputation as an outdoorsy kind of town, most of us don't play sport. A survey by the Bureau of Statistics in 1996 revealed that only 29 per cent of adults in NSW participate in organised physical activities. We love to watch— football and cricket mainly, with basketball for the teens. But actually doing it?

For the athletic minority of men, the most popular games are golf, soccer, lawn bowls and cricket. For women, it's aerobics, netball, tennis and swimming. Sydney kids are a bit healthier— 62 per cent of them play sport through schools or clubs, mainly swimming, netball, basketball, soccer and rugby league. It's this sort of training that has made Australia the world's top swimming and netballing nation.

Sydney's first golf course was set up in 1855 by a Scot, somewhere between Homebush and Concord, probably near the present Concord Golf Club. The oldest still-operating club is the Australian Golf Club,

established at Botany in 1882. Australia has the highest proportion of golf courses per population of any country in the world—one for every 1200 people—and 90 of those courses are in Sydney.

Men's lawn bowls began in Sydney as an organised sport in 1845 and women formed their own association in 1929. The Royal NSW Bowling Association works hard to convince people that the game is not restricted to people over 60.

By contrast, nobody disputes the notion that basketball's prime audience is under 25. In the 1980s we absorbed that passion along with most other details of the culture across the Pacific. The now-regular games at the Sydney Entertainment Centre draw crowds of 12 000, barracking for the Kings (the Sydney men's team) or the Flames (the women's team).

The big event in the tennis season is the NSW Open in December at the eastern suburbs' White City courts—the name is redolent of the glorious 1950s when Sydney-born heroes such as Ken Rosewall and Lew Hoad would regularly capture the Davis Cup there. Sadly, the Australian Open is now held in Melbourne.

50
footy

S ydney's favourite sport got started in 1907 when some of the men who played rugby (a ball game that originated in England's upper class schools early in the 19th century) thought they should be paid more money. They formed a break-away group called the rugby league, leaving the players of the original game to call their group the rugby union. Sydney's first rugby league club was Newtown, formed in 1908. Later that year, South Sydney won the first Sydney premiership.

Rugby league caught the public imagination, presumably because it involves a lot of body contact and the potential for violence. Now the

sport has turned from a series of matches between clubs in New South Wales and Queensland country towns and suburbs into a nationwide moneymaking monster. In 1996 the players split again into two groups: those who worked for Rupert Murdoch's News Corporation in a mass entertainment called Super League, and those who stayed loyal to the traditional club structure under an organisation called the ARL (Australian Rugby League).

Fans now have the choice of watching games amongst ten Super League teams (including ones from Canberra, Newcastle, Adelaide, Perth, Brisbane, North Queensland and New Zealand) or amongst 12 ARL teams (eight Sydney suburban teams plus ones from Newcastle, Illawarra, the Gold Coast and South Queensland).

Rugby union potters along quietly, still primarily as an amateur sport, and so does soccer, with most clubs originating with European immigrants. There has also been an attempt to interest Sydneysiders in the game of Australian Rules—followed obsessively in Melbourne, Adelaide and Perth—with the formation of a team called the Sydney Swans. But none of these has yet had league's power to boost television ratings during the winter and to bring Sydney to flag-waving hysteria in September when the top two teams do battle in the Grand Final at the Sydney Football Stadium (sometimes called the SFS).

Names to know include North Sydney (the Bears), Penrith (the Panthers), Canterbury (the Bulldogs), Manly (the Sea Eagles) and Parramatta (the Eels) and out-of-city intruders, the Brisbane Broncos and the Canberra Raiders. However, there are questions about league's future. Schools are turning to other sports because of the high rate of injuries, which means the clubs will be drawing from a smaller pool of good players. And the arrival of the Super League means splitting the talent between two competitions. Can Sydney stand it?

Some Sydney names to know across the codes:

☆ Herbert 'Dally' Messenger, outstanding kicker and founding father of league in 1908.

☆ Johnny Raper, lock forward for St George Leagues Club in the 1960s.

☆ Artie Beetson, lock forward and captain of Eastern Suburbs Leagues Club in the 1970s.

☆ Mark Ella, rugby union player for Randwick and captain of Australia's international team through the 1980s.

☆ Nick Farr-Jones, brilliant rugby union halfback and Australian captain who retired in 1993.

☆ Paul 'Fatty' Vautin, Manly-Warringah league lock forward in the early 1990s and more recently host of TV's *The Footy Show*.

☆ Peter 'Sterlo' Sterling, halfback for Parramatta Leagues Club during the 1980s and now a TV commentator.

51
cricket

C ricket comes a close second to rugby league as Sydney's top spectator sport. It's been played here since at least January 1804, when a patch of ground called Phillip's Common, now part of Hyde Park, was the scene of Australia's first recorded cricket match. It involved officers from the supply ship *Calcutta* and some free settlers, but no convicts or Aboriginal players.

The first match on the hallowed soil that came to be called the Sydney Cricket Ground was between the Garrison Club and the Royal Victoria Club in 1854. At the time, the space was a playing area for soldiers but it soon became the city's main sports field, used for rugby and athletics as often as cricket. It was officially declared a cricket mecca in 1894 and the stands bear the names of local heroes such as Noble, Bradman and O'Reilly. Between October and March, the SCG hosts Sheffield Shield matches (interstate battles which the NSW Blues have won more often than anybody) and day-and-night matches between various international teams. In January, it's the scene of five-day Test matches—part of a regular round of competitions held between

Australia, England, New Zealand, the West Indies, South Africa, India, Sri Lanka and Pakistan—and the most important event in the cricket buff's calendar.

The Sydney cricketing names to know include:

☆ Ray Lindwall, fast bowler of the late 1940s and 50s who died in 1996.

☆ Richie Benaud, captain of the Australian Test side in the 1950s, now a TV commentator on the game.

☆ Allan Border, Test captain in the 1980s and the highest run scorer in Australian cricket.

☆ Alan McGilvray, captain of the NSW side in the 1930s and then comforting commentator on the game for the ABC until his death in 1996.

☆ Mark Taylor, brilliant batsman of the early 1990s who went on to captain the Australian Test side.

52
gambling

*f*rom the arrival of the British, Sydney has been a city addicted to gambling. Governments have taxed it or banned it with varying degrees of success, and the police have fought it with varying degrees of corruption. The first convicts played 'pitch and toss', which involved betting on the fall of two coins, and in 1805, the *Sydney Gazette* referred to an epidemic of 'chuck-farthing' in the colony. By the end of the 19th century, the name of the game had become 'two-up' and the phrase 'come in spinner' (the instruction to launch the coins into the air) was part of the Sydney vocabulary.

In 1907, a professional boxer named Joe Thomas founded Tommo's two-up school, which kept moving to avoid raids and endured till the 1970s. The game was such a favourite with soldiers returning from both world wars that the authorities declared it could be legally played on just one day of the year—Anzac Day, the public holiday when Australia's military sacrifices are commemorated.

After the Second World War, two-up faded away in the face of more sophisticated games played at illegal casinos, which were occasionally invaded with great theatricality by police who somehow never managed to catch the owners.

Meanwhile, the legal forms of gambling included State-run lotteries, poker machines (legalised in 1956 but restricted to licensed clubs, which used the revenue to turn themselves into entertainment palaces) and racing. The colony's first organised 'race week' was held in Hyde Park in October 1810. Now Sydney has four horse racing venues—Royal Randwick, Canterbury Park, Rosehill Gardens and Warwick Farm—and there's a meeting at one of them every Wednesday and Saturday of the year.

For those who'd rather see horses pulling little carriages, there are Friday night meetings of 'the trots' at Harold Park Paceway, following a tradition that started in Parramatta in 1811. And greyhounds, the most working class form of racing, chase fake rabbits on Friday and Saturday nights at the Wentworth Park track, when optimistic dog owners from the outer western suburbs come to the inner city hoping to change their luck on 'the dogs'.

Taxes on racing earn the NSW government $12 billion a year. From the state's 75 000 poker machines it earns $2 billion, while lotteries make $4 billion. This means that 13 per cent of the state's revenue comes from the money that its citizens and visitors pour into gambling.

53
the casino

*g*rown weary of trying to force the police to close illegal gambling dens, and eager to get access to some of the money spent in them, the NSW government in the late 1980s decided to legalise more forms of gambling—but only at one giant casino to be built at Darling Harbour. Australia's richest man, Kerry Packer, applied for the licence to run it, but for once, he lost. It was given to the Leighton's consortium that included the experienced American casino operator Showboat.

Construction of this palace proceeded through the 1990s, and in mid 1997, the Sydney Harbour Casino announced that, after market research, it would change its name to Star City. This was meant to indicate the diverse entertainments within the complex, but critics said it sounded 'more crass than class'. It seemed to confirm a sense of second-rateness that Sydneysiders felt when they learned they had been trumped by the opening of a new casino on the bank of the Yarra River in Melbourne.

Recognising Problem Gamblers

Mr Jones, wonderful to see you here again! We've kept a seat free at your usual table

Here's a comparison:

From 1998, Sydney's Star City will have a 500-room hotel, 2500 underground car parking spaces, 200 gaming tables, 1500 poker machines, two theatres, one nightclub, 12 restaurants, 10 bars, a range of high-tech rides for the kids and 5000 staff. It hopes for 20 000 visitors a day and annual revenue of $500 million.

Melbourne's Crown Casino will have a 1000-room hotel, 5400 parking spaces, 350 gaming tables, 2500 poker machines, two theatres, three nightclubs, 35 restaurants, 17 bars and cafes, 14 cinemas and 8000 staff. It hopes for 40 000 visitors a day and annual revenue of $1 billion. Still, Sydney wouldn't want the kind of visitor who'd go to a city purely for a glitzy casino. Would we?

STIMULATION

54
radio

a ustralia's first radio station started broadcasting in Sydney in December 1923. It was
called 2SB but later changed its name to 2BL and
became part of the advertisement-free, government-
funded ABC network. Nowadays 2BL provides
news, current affairs, talkback, sport and a little
music. It competes strongly with about 30 AM and
FM commercial stations in Sydney, attracting
about 9 per cent of the listening audience, and it
offers a politically-balanced viewpoint where most
other talk stations are conservative. It can be found
at 702 on the AM dial.

Sydney's most successful station, with 13 per cent
of the audience, is 2UE (954 AM). It offers talk and
sports and its opinion leaders are Alan Jones (breakfast announcer with strong links to the Liberal
Party) and John Laws
(morning announcer who
encourages listeners to buy
his associated products,
particularly books of wise
sayings). They are influential enough to be courted
by politicians and they elicit

I'd just like to say, Phil,
that I love your program

And I'd like to say that
you're a crawling liar,
but I can't,
we're on air

a love/hate response among Sydneysiders.

2KY (1017 AM) attracts the red-necked racing crowd while 2EA (SBS-radio on 1386 AM) is a tower of Babel representing many of the non-English languages spoken in Sydney.

The most interesting young music station is 2JJJ (105.7 FM), nationally broadcast on the ABC, while 2MMM (104.9 FM) offers hard rock and 2DAY (104.1 FM) offers pop for the over 25s. The best 60s rock-n-roll appears on 2WS (101.7 FM) which specialises in news for people in Sydney's western suburbs. For people over 50, 2CH (1170 AM) offers gentle music and a little news.

Serious music buffs can choose between the ABC's Classic FM (92.6 FM) and the volunteer-run 2MBS (102.5 FM) which occasionally interrupts its music to make appeals for donations. Serious talk buffs can devote themselves to ABC's Radio National (576 AM) which analyses life's issues from a leftish perspective.

55
television

*a*ll Australian TV networks have their head-quarters in Sydney, which may be why they rarely set programs here—to avoid displaying a hometown bias.

The classic series about Sydney was *Number 96*, a sexy soap opera supposedly set in a Paddington apartment block but actually set in the Moncur apartments, 83 Moncur Street, Woollahra. When it began in 1972, the critics declared that Australian television had 'lost its virginity'. That was because the show had sympathetic characters who were promiscuous, gay, immigrant or wine drinkers—standard Sydney types, in fact. More recently the soap *Home and Away* has been filmed around Palm Beach but it pretends to be set in a coastal town called Summer Bay, and the cop series *Water Rats* has been set around Sydney Harbour.

The broadcast TV stations available in Sydney are:
☆ SBS (partly funded by the federal government, with occasional commercials) which specialises in foreign language programs.

151

☆ Two (run by the federal government-funded ABC) which specialises in news, British comedies, Australian drama and documentaries.

☆ Nine, which shows US dramas and sitcoms and a lot of Australian sport.

☆ Ten, which aims for a groovier audience and shows *Seinfeld* and *The Simpsons*.

☆ Seven, which aims somewhere between Ten and Nine, and has Australia's most popular show, *Blue Heelers* (set in a country town in Victoria).

There are also numerous pay-TV stations but their content is mostly American and very few people subscribe to them. Sydney's best-known TV performers are Ray Martin, a charmer with gappy teeth who presents *A Current Affair* on Nine; Kerry-Anne Kennerley, a big-haired blonde who presents *The Midday Show* on Nine; Brian Henderson, bland and bespectacled, who reads the Nine news; the terribly serious Jana Wendt, formerly of *60 Minutes*, *A Current Affair* and Seven's program *Witness*, which she left after a fight over her role in determining the content; bearded Don Burke, who probes into people's lives via their gardening habits in a show called *Burke's Backyard*; Monica Trapaga, a sexy *Play School* presenter; the Wiggles, a pop band for the under 5's and cherubic Indira Naidoo, an ABC news presenter with a nice manner who has become a gay icon.

STIMULATION

56
regular reading

S ydney's major newspapers are:
☆ **THE DAILY TELEGRAPH.** A lively and
surprisingly accurate tabloid owned by Rupert
Murdoch, which sells about 440 000 copies
each weekday. Its editorial policy and most of
its columnists are conservative, but it offers a
thorough coverage of local crime and
international showbiz. Its sister, *The Sunday
Telegraph*, is Australia's biggest-selling paper,
at over 710 000 copies a week.

☆ **THE SYDNEY MORNING HERALD.** A more
thoughtful analyst of politics and business,
which sells about 237 000 copies each weekday
and 410 000 copies of its fat Saturday edition
(containing the classified ads that many Sydney
people use to seek jobs and buy houses and
cars). Its most useful
supplements are a TV
guide on Mondays, a
restaurant and cooking
guide called Good
Living on Tuesdays, and
an entertainment guide
called Metro on Fridays.

The paper was founded in 1840 by the Fairfax family but the company fell out of the family's hands in the late 1980s when one of its younger members, Warwick, went broke in a bizarre attempt to take over the company from within. A favourite media joke goes: Q. 'How do you start a small business in Sydney?' A. 'Give a *big* business to Warwick Fairfax'.

☆ **THE AUSTRALIAN.** A serious national daily owned by Rupert Murdoch, which sells 120 000 copies Australia-wide each weekday and more than 310 000 on Saturday.

☆ **THE AUSTRALIAN FINANCIAL REVIEW.** A Monday to Friday national business paper produced by the Fairfax company, which sells 88 000 copies a day Australia-wide.

While Sydneysiders are solid newspaper readers, they share with other Australians a passion for magazines that specialise in showbiz gossip and astrology. The biggest sellers are *Women's Weekly* (about 889 000 copies a month nationally) and *Woman's Day* (about 754 000 copies a week nationally). Both are owned by Australia's richest man, Kerry Packer, whose firm Australian Consolidated Press is based in Sydney.

57
cinemas

Sydney's first moving pictures were shown at the Tivoli Theatre in Castlereagh Street in 1896 when a magician called Carl Hertz included them in his act. They were so popular that entrepreneurs started adapting playhouses and concert halls to make movie-showing an option. Sydney's first purpose-built cinema seems to have been the 1911 Lyric Wintergarden in George Street near Railway Square, and George Street has remained a cinema strip ever since.

In the 1920s—the period of Sydney's greatest wealth—there was intense competition to create Australia's most lavish cinemas. Most of those extravagances have since been pulled down, but the State Theatre in Market Street remains, recently refurbished to its 1929 red and gold gothic glory. It is now the site of the annual Sydney Film Festival in June, as well as live concerts. The former TV presenter Mike Walsh has done Sydney a service by refurbishing the art deco Orpheum Picture Palace in Military Road, Cremorne, where a mighty wurlitzer organ rises from the floor to entertain patrons before the features begin.

Mainstream movies can now be seen in the

multiplex cinemas along George Street between Bathurst and Liverpool Streets, and around the suburbs. More unusual films—from arthouse ephemera to cult classics—are shown at the three Dendy Cinemas (Martin Place, George Street, or Newtown); the Verona, the Academy Twin and the Chauvel, all in Oxford Street, Paddington; the Walker Street in North Sydney; and the Valhalla in Glebe Point Road, Glebe.

STIMULATION

58
films about Sydney

*W*ay back in 1959, an obscure American actor called Aldo Ray starred in a film called *The Siege of Pinchgut* (the colloquial name for Fort Denison, an island in the middle of Sydney Harbour). He played the leader of a gang who trained cannons at a ship containing bombs, and held Sydney to ransom (a plot which must have inspired the more recent film, *The Rock*). Seeing it as a child, I was proud to think that my city had finally become a subject for international film-makers. So far as I can find out, that was the first time Sydney had provided the central plotline of a movie designed primarily for British and American audiences (even if its title was changed to *Four Desperate Men* when it was shown over there).

Since that time, Australia has rebuilt its own film industry and Sydney has provided the backdrop for countless movies. Here are some of them.

☆ *They're A Weird Mob* (1966), a comedy about how strange Sydney looks to immigrants.

☆ *Caddie* (1976) with Helen Morse as a single mother forced to work as a barmaid in the 1930s. Scenes were shot around Burwood.

☆ *The Last Wave* (1977), a Peter Weir film with Richard Chamberlain as a visitor who gets spooked by Aboriginal legends at Bondi Beach.

☆ *Palm Beach* (1980) with Bryan Brown as a bungling robber, operating in the surf and drug culture of the northern beaches.

☆ *Puberty Blues* (1981) with Nell Schofield as a surfie chick on Cronulla beach.

☆ *Winter of our Dreams* (1981) with Judy Davis as a junkie prostitute who leaves Kings Cross to involve herself with a Balmain writer played by Bryan Brown.

☆ *Heatwave* (1982) with Judy Davis as yet another version of Juanita Nielsen fighting developers in central Sydney.

☆ *Star Struck* (1982), an early Gillian Armstrong effort about teens singing and dancing in the Palisades Hotel at the Rocks.

☆ *BMX Bandits* (1983) with a teenage Nicole Kidman biking round the northern beaches.

☆ *Careful He Might Hear You* (1983) with Wendy Hughes as an upper class bitch in the 1920s. It contrasts posh suburbs with working class suburbs and ends with the sinking of the ferry *Greycliffe* in the Harbour.

☆ *The Coca Cola Kid* (1985) with Greta Scacchi

as a sex object. Filmed around inner Sydney and the Blue Mountains.

☆ *The Empty Beach* (1985) with Bryan Brown as private eye Cliff Hardy. It was filmed around Bondi and Tamarama.

☆ *Mad Max Beyond Thunderdome* (1985) with Mel Gibson as the loner hero leading a bunch of feral children to post-apocalyptic Sydney harbour (without water).

☆ *Rebel* (1985) with Matt Dillon as an American soldier who falls in love with Debbie Byrne in Kings Cross in 1942.

☆ *Emerald City* (1989) with John Hargreaves as a Melbourne playwright who moves to Sydney to write film scripts and fancies Nicole Kidman. Harbour views, scenes inside the State Theatre.

☆ *Sweetie* (1989), Jane Campion's first feature, with Genevieve Lemon as a loony. Filmed in Sydney suburbs so drab they look like Melbourne.

☆ *The Last Days of Chez Nous* (1992), a Gillian Armstrong film with Lisa Harrow as a writer having trouble with her lover and her sister. Filmed around Glebe.

☆ *Strictly Ballroom* (1992), Baz Luhrmann's first feature with Paul Mercurio as a flamenco dancer. Partly filmed around Ultimo.

☆ *The Nostradamus Kid* (1993) with Noah Taylor as the writer Bob Ellis going to Sydney University in the 1960s.

☆ *The Adventures of Priscilla, Queen of the Desert* (1994), about female impersonators going bush. It begins and ends in the gay pubs of Newtown.

☆ *The Custodian* (1994) with Anthony LaPaglia as a city cop rooting out corruption.

☆ *Muriel's Wedding* (1994) with Toni Collette as a small town girl who finds life's meaning in the big city.

☆ *The Sum of Us* (1994) with Jack Thompson as a straight ferry captain and Russell Crowe as his gay plumber son, sharing a house in Balmain.

☆ *Billy's Holiday* (1995) with Max Cullen as a jazz singer whose voice goes high. Filmed around Newtown.

☆ *Mr Reliable* (1996), a reconstruction of a 1968 siege in the outer western suburbs.

☆ *Lilian's Story* (1996) with Ruth Cracknell as the 1950s Sydney eccentric Bea Miles.

☆ *Independence Day* (1996), which contains a glimpse of Sydney Harbour after an alien-induced firestorm.

☆ *Napoleon* (1996), in which a dog journeys from the Harbour to the desert and back.

☆ *Children of the Revolution* (1997) with Judy Davis as a Balmain communist who sleeps with Stalin.

☆ *Idiot Box* (1997) with Ben Mendelsohn and Jeremy Sims as would-be bank robbers in the western suburbs.

59
theatre

*t*he Aboriginal people of the Port Jackson area had engaged in song and dance performances for thousands of years before Europeans arrived, but the first written record of a show performed in Sydney concerns the night of 4 June 1789. On that occasion some 60 people sat down to commemorate the birthday of King George III and watched a comedy written in 1706 called *The Recruiting Officer*. It was acted by convicts and the set was decorated with candles.

Sydney's first theatre opened in 1796, run by Robert Sidaway, an ex-convict who had become the colony's official baker. Its shows sparked such enthusiasm among the convicts that they took to stealing to buy tickets, causing Governor Hunter to order the theatre's closure in 1798. When the town was a little more mature—in 1833—the first professional theatre opened in a warehouse beside the Royal Hotel in the mid city. But stage shows didn't really become a mass entertainment till the 1880s, when an American actor named James Cassius Williamson set up a circuit of theatres in Sydney, Melbourne, Adelaide and Brisbane, featuring overseas performers on tour. After his death in 1913, the

J C Williamson chain became known as 'The Firm'.

Williamson's was replaced in the 1950s by the Australian Elizabethan Theatre Trust, which set up opera, ballet and drama companies across the nation and encouraged local artists. Its opera company took the name The Australian Opera in 1962, and based itself in Sydney. Its home became the Sydney Opera House in 1973, and throughout the 1970s Dame Joan Sutherland was a regular guest star. Nowadays, it's the third largest opera company in the world, employing 280 people full time and performing in the Opera House nine months of the year (disappearing to Melbourne from March to May).

The NSW government started funding the Sydney Theatre Company in 1984 and gave it a home in one of the old wharves at Walsh Bay, near Circular Quay, renovated to provide rehearsal spaces and two theatres. The STC occasionally does international hit plays, but it emphasises the work of local authors, particularly David Williamson. It uses the Opera House's Drama Theatre for some of its productions.

The three main commercial theatres in town are Her Majesty's near Central Railway, The Theatre Royal in King Street, and the Capitol in the Haymarket. They stay dark for much of the year and occasionally feature Andrew Lloyd Webber musicals or revivals of shows such as *West Side Story*. More experimental theatre is done at the

Belvoir in Surry Hills and Griffin at the Stables in Darlinghurst. The suburban live theatres—The Ensemble at North Sydney, Marian Street at Killara, the Q Theatre at Penrith and Glen Street at French Forest—tend to stick with safe overseas successes.

The Sydney Dance Company was founded in 1979 by Graeme Murphy. About once a year it suddenly appears with an exciting modern program, often choreographed by Murphy. It produced Paul Mercurio, who was briefly known as the star of *Strictly Ballroom*. The Bangarra Aboriginal dance company, which mixes traditional movement with modern styles, is also based in Sydney.

Names to know in Sydney theatre include:

☆ John Bell, creative force in the Bell Shakespeare Company
☆ Cate Blanchett, serious young actress
☆ Kate Fitzpatrick, actress in the Mae West vein
☆ Drew Forsythe, comic actor
☆ Hayes Gordon, a US born musical comedy star who set up the Ensemble Studios in North Sydney
☆ Barrie Kosky, provocative director
☆ Richard Roxburgh, serious actor
☆ Richard Wherrett, flamboyant director, often with the Sydney Theatre Company.

60
music

i t's a pub rock town and an orchestral town. It's not much of a jazz town but, since the 1990s, it's become quite an a cappella town.

☆ **THE CLASSICS.** Sydney decided to take music seriously in 1908, when the Government House stables (built in 1821) were transformed into the Conservatorium of Music, to present concerts and train musicians. A bunch of graduates from 'the Con' formed the Sydney Symphony Orchestra in 1932, but they didn't get a full-time, government-paid conductor until 1947. He was Sir Eugene Goossens and his greatest contribution to Sydney was persuading the state government that the old tramsheds site on Bennelong Point would be an ideal spot to create an opera house. However, Goossens left Sydney in 1956 before he could even see the plans for the building he inspired—he'd been caught by the customs people returning from an overseas visit with pornography in his suitcase.

The Sydney Symphony Orchestra grew to become one of the world's busiest. Their home is the concert hall of the Sydney Opera House and they perform more than 150 concerts a year, heard by 200 000 people. Most Christmases, the SSO joins with the hundreds of voices in the Sydney Philharmonia Choir to present a version of Handel's *Messiah*, and that's a sound to hear.

Meanwhile, in 1945, an entrepreneur named Richard Goldner used the profits from his invention called the Triplex Fastener to start the organisation Musica Viva, arranging chamber music concerts by local and overseas artists. It now promotes some 2000 performances a year across the country, with its best-known product being the Australian Chamber Orchestra, based in Sydney and often performing in the Opera House, the Town Hall or the Seymour Centre near Sydney University.

☆ **ROCK.** During the 1960s, a number of Sydney publicans decided that the way to attract younger customers was to let local imitators of the Rolling Stones play in their biggest drinking rooms. To keep the audience's attention, the bands had to be fast and loud. This became a Sydney tradition and a tough training ground for such groups as Cold Chisel, AC/DC, Midnight Oil and the Angels. Nowadays, the liveliest rock is likely to be found in the Sandringham Hotel, 387

We've warned nightclubbers of the damage being done to their hearing, but do you think they listen?!

165

King Street, Newtown; the Annandale
Hotel, corner of Nelson Street and Parramatta
Road, Annandale; Selina's, within the Coogee
Bay Hotel on the corner of Arden Street and
Coogee Bay Road, Coogee; The Bridge Hotel,
135 Victoria Road, Rozelle; the Cat & Fiddle
Hotel, 456 Darling Street, Balmain; and the
Hopetoun Hotel, 416 Bourke Street, Surry
Hills. A less chaotic venue for experienced
bands is the Metro at 624 George Street in the
city.

☆ **JAZZ.** It can be found in the smoke-free rooms
of The Basement, 29 Reiby Place, near Circular
Quay or at the Harbourside Brasserie in Pier
One at Millers Point. For blues and folkie stuff,
there's the Rose Shamrock and Thistle (better
known as The Three Weeds), 193 Evans Street,
Rozelle.

☆ **A CAPPELLA.** This form of harmony singing
without musical instruments became a fad in
Sydney in the early 1990s, with its best-known
practitioners being the Choir at the Cafe at the
Gates of Salvation. Sub-groups of this choir
sing all over the city, and the best way to hear
their music—or to join them—is to phone the
Sydney Acappella Association on 9144 5501.

☆ **RECORD STORES.** The big mainstream stores
are Blockbuster, HMV and Brash's, all in Pitt
Street in midtown, but there are specialist
music stores throughout the inner city. For

classics, there's Michael's Music Room, Shop 19, Town Hall Arcade. For jazz, there's Birdland, 3 Barrack Street. For hard-to-find older pop, there's Time Warp, 289 Clarence Street. For obscure recent rock, try Red Eye in the Tankstream Arcade, corner of King and Pitt Streets. And for second-hand stuff, there's Ashwoods, 376 Pitt Street. At 282 Oxford Street, Paddington, you'll find Folkways—a good source for folk, jazz, some classics and a fair bit of rock.

☆ **NAMES TO KNOW IN SYDNEY MUSIC.** Here's a long list which is by no means definitive: **Little Pattie** Amphlett, 60s singer of *He's My Blonde Headed Stompy Wompie Real Gone Surfer Boy*; **John Antill**, classical composer who wrote the ballet suite *Corroboree* in 1944; **Don Burrows**, player of jazz flute, clarinet and saxophone and, during the 1980s, director of jazz studies at the Con; **Stuart Challender**, conductor of the Sydney Symphony Orchestra who in 1991 went public with the news that he had AIDS; **Iva Davies**, composer and former singer with Icehouse, whose hits included *Great Southern Land* and *Electric Blue* in the 80s; **The Delltones**, 60s surfer group whose bass singer Pee Wee Wilson continues the tradition; **Jon English**, who found fame as Judas in *Jesus Christ Superstar* in the early 70s, had hit singles in the late 70s with

167

Six Ribbons and *Words Are Not Enough*, did TV comedy and now appears in updated Gilbert and Sullivan musicals; **Joan Hammond**, NSW golf champion in the 30s, world famous soprano in the 40s, singing teacher since the 60s; **Marcia Hines**, an American soul singer who came here to star in *Hair* in 1970 and stayed, producing an equally musical daughter **Deni**; **Vince Jones**, cool jazz singer; **Richard Meale**, classical composer best known for the operas *Voss* and *Mer de Glace*; **James Morrison**, jazz trumpeter and flute player; **Johnny O'Keefe**, rock and roller of the 60s, known as The Wild One, with hits such as *She's My Baby* and *Move Baby Move*; **Marilyn Richardson**, soprano, particularly good at Wagner; **Peter Sculthorpe**, classical composer best known for *Sun Music*; **Barry Tuckwell**, Sydney-trained classical trumpeter and conductor, now based in London; **You Am I**, Sydney's pre-eminent rock band of the mid 90s.

61
writing

*t*he first book published in Australia was *New South Wales General Standing Orders*, printed by George Howe in 1802, but the first book written by someone born in Australia was *A Statistical, Historical and Political Description of the Colony of New South Wales* by William Charles Wentworth in 1819. Some 170 years later, the NSW government has set up a 'writers walk' around Circular Quay in which authors with relevance to Sydney are commemorated by bronze plaques in the ground. They include:

☆ **PETER CAREY.** Born in Melbourne in 1943, Carey ran an advertising agency in Sydney during the 1970s while writing fantasy stories, and then won the Miles Franklin Award for his novel *Bliss* in 1982, and the Booker Prize for *Oscar and Lucinda* in 1988. He now lives in New York but worries about Australia.

☆ **PETER CORRIS.** Born in 1942 and trained as a historian, he began writing thrillers in 1980. His best-known novels—such as *The Dying Trade* and *The Empty Beach*—concern the troubled Balmain private eye Cliff Hardy.

☆ **MILES FRANKLIN.** Born near Tumut, NSW, she wrote her first novel (*My Brilliant Career*) in 1901 when she was 20, then got involved in feminist politics in Sydney, New York and London. She returned to Sydney in 1932, wrote a portrait of suburban life called *All That Swagger* (1936) and endowed an annual prize for a novel depicting Australian life, which became the country's most prestigious literary award. She published *My Career Goes Bung* in 1946 and died in 1954.

☆ **MAY GIBBS.** Born in England in 1876, she settled in Sydney and, in 1916, published *The Gumnut Babies*, a set of children's stories using bush imagery. It started a series about Snugglepot and Cuddlepie and the Big Bad Banksia Men, who became the first homegrown folklore for three generations of Australian children.

☆ **CLIVE JAMES.** Born in Kogarah in 1939 and now a London TV presenter, James offered this portrait in his autobiography *Unreliable Memoirs* (1980): 'In Sydney Harbour, the yachts will be racing on the crushed diamond water under a sky the texture of powered sapphires. It would be churlish not to concede that the same abundance of natural blessings which gave us the energy to leave has every right to call us back.'

☆ **GEORGE JOHNSTON.** Born in Melbourne in

1912, Johnston became a journalist for the *Sydney Sun* newspaper and in the 1960s wrote the novels *My Brother Jack* and *Clean Straw for Nothing*, from which comes this: 'Sydney is a city of light and wind more than of architecture ... The majesties of nature and the monstrosities of man have a cheek by jowl evidence in Sydney more insistent, I think, than in any other city in the world.'

☆ **THOMAS KENEALLY.** Born in 1935, he trained for the Catholic priesthood before turning to writing. His novels include *Bring Larks and Heroes* (1967, a Miles Franklin Award winner), *The Chant of Jimmy Blacksmith* (1972) and *Schindler's Ark* (which won the Booker Prize in 1982 and became the film *Schindler's List*).

☆ **RUDYARD KIPLING.** The author of *The Jungle Book* visited Sydney in 1937 and wrote this description in *Something of Myself*: 'Sydney was populated by leisured multitudes all in their shirt sleeves and all picnicking all the day. They volunteered that they were new and young, but would do wonderful things some day.'

☆ **HENRY LAWSON.** Born in 1867 in Grenfell, NSW, he moved to Sydney in 1883 with his social activist mother and began to write poems, stories and political arguments, particularly for Australia becoming a republic.

His best story collection is *Joe Wilson and his Mates* (1901).

☆ **DOROTHEA MACKELLAR.** She's remembered for one poem, *My Country* (originally called *Core of My Heart*), written in 1904 when she was 19. It includes: 'I love a sunburnt country, a land of sweeping plains'.

☆ **DAVID MALOUF.** Born in Brisbane in 1934, he now lives in Sydney. Malouf's novels—often about Australian identity—include *Johnno* (1975), *The Great World* (1991, a Miles Franklin Award winner) and *Remembering Babylon* (1993).

☆ **RUTH PARK.** Born in New Zealand in 1923, she chronicled life in the Sydney slums with the novels *A Harp in the South* (1947) and *Poor Man's Orange* (1949). Her plaque contains this quote from her guide to Sydney: 'To walk into the Opera House is to walk inside a sculpture, or perhaps a seashell, maybe an intricate half-translucent nautilus.'

☆ **ANDREW 'BANJO' PATERSON.** Born in 1864 near Orange, NSW, Australia's bush balladist worked as a solicitor in Sydney while writing *Clancy of the Overflow* and *The Man From Snowy River* (1895). From *It's Grand* (1902) comes this image: 'It's grand to be unemployed/And lie in the Domain; /And wake up every second day—/ and go to sleep again.'

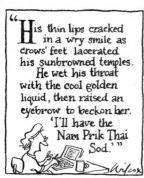

"His thin lips cracked in a wry smile as crows' feet lacerated his sunbrowned temples. He wet his throat with the cool golden liquid, then raised an eyebrow to beckon her. 'I'll have the Nam Prik Thai Sod.'"

☆ **KENNETH SLESSOR.** A poet obsessed with Sydney Harbour and Kings Cross, his triumph was a poem called *Five Bells* in 1939. His turreted house in Billyard Avenue, Elizabeth Bay is a literary landmark.

☆ **CHRISTINA STEAD.** Born in 1902, she spent most of her adult life in London or Hollywood but wrote *Seven Poor Men of Sydney* in 1934 and then such international successes as *The Man Who Loved Children* (1941) and *For Love Alone* (1944). She returned to live in Sydney from 1974 until her death in 1983.

☆ **KYLIE TENNANT.** Born in 1912, she chronicled Sydney poverty in novels like *The Battlers* (1941) and *Tell Morning This* (1967) and is best known for *Ride On Stranger* (1943).

☆ **PATRICK WHITE.** Born in England in 1912 of an Australian grazier family, White lived most of his life in Sydney and won the Nobel Prize for Literature in 1973, for 'the first time giving the continent of Australia an authentic voice that carries across the world'. His novels include The *Tree of Man* (1955), *Voss* (1957) and *The Eye of the Storm* (1973).

☆ **DAVID WILLIAMSON.** Australia's pre-eminent playwright, he was born in Melbourne in 1942, moved to Sydney as an adult, and wrote such plays as *The Removalists* (1972), *Don's Party* (1973), and *Money and Friends* (1991) and such film scripts as *Gallipoli* (1981) and *Phar Lap* (1983). In *Emerald City* (1987) he made this observation: 'In Melbourne all views are equally depressing, so there is no point in having one . . . No-one in Sydney ever wastes time debating the meaning of life—it's getting yourself a water frontage. People devote a lifetime to the quest.'

☆ **JUDITH WRIGHT.** She's Australia's greatest female poet, and an activist for conservation and Aboriginal rights. Her works include *The Moving Image* (1946), *Woman To Man* (1949), *Five Senses* (1963) and *Fourth Quartet* (1976).

Other notable Sydney writers not yet commemorated on the walk include:

☆ **PHILIP ADAMS.** More prolific and more opinionated than is healthy for anyone, he writes two weekly columns for *The Australian* newspaper, presents a nightly ABC radio talk show and publishes bestsellers such as *The Penguin Book of Australian Jokes*. He's also been a film producer and successful lobbyist for government funding of the arts.

☆ **ALEX BUZO.** Born in 1944, he wrote plays such as *Rooted* (1969) and *Makassar Reef*

(1978), and became a commentator on linguistic curiosities such as tautology and New Zealand pronunciation.

☆ **MANNING CLARK.** Born in 1915, he wrote *A History of Australia* in six volumes between 1962 and 1987, expressing sympathy for the underdogs. After his death in 1991, he was accused of supporting Soviet communism.

☆ **BRYCE COURTENAY.** Born in South Africa, now resident in Sydney, he's Australia's best-selling novelist, concentrating in the mid 1990s on an Australian historical trilogy that begins with *The Potato Factory*.

☆ **ROBERT DREWE.** A journalist turned novelist, he's obsessed with the beach in Australian culture, as you may gather from his titles—*Our Sunshine* (1991), *The Bodysurfers* (1993) and *The Drowner* (1996).

☆ **SUMNER LOCKE ELLIOTT.** He wrote a hit play called *Rusty Bugles* in 1948, moved to America to write TV scripts in the 1950s, and produced three novels about Australia: *Careful He Might Hear You* (1963), *Edens Lost* (1969) and *Water Under The Bridge* (1977).

☆ **DONALD HORNE.** He wrote social commentaries called *The Lucky Country* (1964) and *Death of the Lucky Country* (1976) and now campaigns for reform, particularly republicanism in Australia.

☆ **DAVID IRELAND.** He has won the Miles Franklin Award three times for his novels *An Unknown Industrial Prisoner* (1971), *The Glass Canoe* (1976) and *A Woman of the Future* (1979).

☆ **HENRY KENDALL.** Before Banjo Patterson, he was Australia's bush poet laureate of the late 19th century, best remembered for *Bell Birds* and *September in Australia.*

☆ **FRANK MOORHOUSE.** He's a former journalist whose short stories such as *The Coca Cola Kid* and *The Everlasting Secret Family* made him king of the Balmain literary ghetto in the early 1980s. His *Days of Wine and Rage* is the definitive portrait of Sydney society in the 1970s. In 1994 Moorhouse took legal action (unsuccessfully) against the judges of the Miles Franklin Award after they excluded his novel *Grand Days* from contention because it was not primarily about Australia.

☆ **JOHN O'GRADY.** Under the pseudonym Nino Culotta, he wrote *They're A Weird Mob* (1957), *Cop This Lot* (1960), and *Gone Fishin'* (1962) about Sydney life through the eyes of a recent immigrant.

☆ **DAVE WARNER.** Originally a rock singer from Perth, he produced two thriller novels, *City of Light* (1995) and *Big Bad Blood* (1996) which impeccably analysed police corruption in the inner city during the Askin era.

62 artists

*a*ustralia's first oil painting was 'A Direct North General View of Sydney Cove' done in 1794 by a Scottish convict named Thomas Watling. He'd been transported for forgery but was able to turn his talents to more socially acceptable uses. It is now owned by the Mitchell Library in Sydney and they'll let you see it if you phone and make an appointment.

Sydney became Australia's portraiture capital in 1922 when the first Archibald Prize was awarded. It had been endowed by Jules Archibald, who founded the *Bulletin* magazine in 1880 and edited it for 25 years. When he died in 1919 he left money so that the Art Gallery of NSW could give an annual award for the best portrait of someone notable in the arts. The Archibald is Australia's dominant art prize and it can greatly boost the asking price for its winners' works.

Prominent artists associated with Sydney include:

☆ **JULIAN ASHTON,** a landscape painter who founded the city's most influential art school in 1895.

☆ **CHARLES BLACKMAN,** a figure painter who studied at East Sydney Technical College and became controversial in the 1950s for his images of schoolgirls.

☆ **JUDY CASSAB,** an expressionist portraitist, born in Vienna, who won the Archibald Prize in 1960 and 1967.

☆ **CHARLES CONDER,** an impressionist landscape painter best known for 'The Departure of the *SS Orient*—Circular Quay' (1887), is now in the Art Gallery of NSW.

☆ **GRACE COSSINGTON SMITH,** a modernist painter of interiors, with a flair for light, best known for 'The Sock Knitter' (1915).

☆ **ROY DE MAISTRE,** the pioneer of post-impressionism and cubism during the 1920s.

☆ **WILLIAM DOBELL,** a portraitist trained at the Julian Ashton School, best known for the controversy over his Archibald Prize-winning portrait of fellow artist Joshua Smith in 1943. Two other artists took a court case claiming the painting was not eligible for the prize because it was a caricature instead of a portrait. They lost, and Dobell went on to win Archibalds again in 1948 and 1959.

☆ **RUSSELL DRYSDALE,** a landscapist who showed the bleakness of Australian outback life between the 1940s and the 1960s.

☆ **DONALD FRIEND,** a traditional figurative artist best known for scenes of Balinese people in the 1970s.

☆ **SALI HERMAN,** a Swiss-born painter of

Sydney urban scenes, best known for 'Potts Point' (1957).

☆ **LIVINGSTONE HOPKINS,** better known as the cartoonist 'Hop', who drew for the *Bulletin* between 1883 and 1905 and started an artists' camp at Balmoral with Julian Ashton.

☆ **COLIN LANCELEY,** an abstract painter who likes to make his work three-dimensional by sticking objects onto the canvas, as with 'Glad Family Picnic' (1962) which seems to satirise littering.

☆ **MARGO LEWERS,** an abstract painter and fabric designer of the 1930s to 50s, whose home and collection was donated to the city of Penrith to start a local art gallery.

☆ **NORMAN LINDSAY,** a cartoonist for the *Bulletin* early this century, a painter of voluptuous women at his home in Springwood in the Blue Mountains, and also the author and illustrator of an iconographic Australian book called *The Magic Pudding* (1918).

☆ **CONRAD MARTENS,** an English painter who arrived in Sydney in 1834 with Charles Darwin, and over the next 35 years produced drawings, watercolours and oil paintings of life around the Harbour—

the first detailed record of what we looked like last century.

☆ **JOHN OLSEN,** abstract expressionist and tapestry designer whose giant mural *Salute to Five Bells* (1973) is in the Sydney Opera House.

☆ **MARGARET PRESTON,** painter and engraver of still lifes with flowers, often with Aboriginal influences, who died in 1963. Her 'Western Australian Gum Blossom' (1928) hangs in the Art Gallery of NSW.

☆ **LLOYD REES,** landscapist and etcher, often of Sydney Harbour scenes, between 1920 and his death in 1988.

☆ **JEFFREY SMART,** a hyper-realist painter of landscapes and city scenes, best known for 'Cahill Expressway' (1962) .

☆ **JOSHUA SMITH,** portraitist who won the Archibald in 1944 but who is best known for being 'caricatured' by William Dobell in 1943 and for never speaking to Dobell again.

☆ **NIGEL THOMPSON,** painter of alarming hyper-realist scenes and portraits, who won the Archibald in 1983 and 1997.

☆ **BRETT WHITELEY,** a landscape artist as famous for his heroin addiction as for his lavish blue scenes of Sydney Harbour and his two Archibald Prizes. He died in 1992 and his studio at 2 Raper Street, Surry Hills, is now a museum.

63
museums

*t*he first 'collection of Australian curiosities' was put on display in 1830 in the office of Sydney's Judge-Advocate and was initially called the Colonial Museum. When it grew unmanageably large, this collection of rocks, bones, tools, stuffed animals and insects moved to a site on the corner of William and College Streets which, when it opened to the public in 1858, was called The Australian Museum. It's been there ever since and remains the biggest natural history collection in the country. Nowadays, it also emphasises Aboriginal history and culture, and enthrals children with dinosaur displays and a room full of skeletons, some of them moving.

In addition, Sydney has developed a range of other museums for every taste, housing both permanent collections and a changing selection of local and international exhibitions. Here's a sampling, starting with the mainstream:

☆ **POWERHOUSE MUSEUM,** 500 Harris Street, Ultimo (9217 0111). This is Australia's biggest museum. It specialises in technology, design, social history and popular culture, and has lots of hands-on gadgetry.

☆ **NATIONAL MARITIME MUSEUM,**
2 Murray Street, Darling Harbour (9552 7777).
It contains—hanging up inside or floating
outside—a Russian submarine, a warship
called *Vampire*, the *Tu Du* (a battered
launch which brought 33 Vietnamese refugees
to Darwin in 1977) and *Australia II* (the
yacht which won the America's Cup in
1983).

☆ **MUSEUM OF CONTEMPORARY ART,**
George Street, the Rocks (9252 4033). It's
primarily a large gallery for poppy/oppy sort of
stuff and modern Aboriginal works.

☆ **MUSEUM OF SYDNEY,** 37 Phillip Street in
the city (9251 5988). Built on the site of the
first Government House, this small museum
looks smart but is poorly signposted so that
only people already well-informed about
Sydney's history can gain a lot from it. It
concentrates on the Eora people who lived
around the Harbour and on the early years
of European settlement.

And here are some museums for more specific
areas of curiosity:

☆ **KIDSEUM,** Pitt and Walpole Streets,
Merrylands (9897 1414). Hands-on play areas
including a doctor's surgery and a TV studio.

☆ **CHRISTMAS MUSEUM GALLERY,**
37 Garfield Road, Horsley Park (9620 1218).
Some 400 nativity scenes from 50 countries,

made of tortoiseshell, gold, ebony, maize leaves and other materials.

☆ **SYDNEY JEWISH MUSEUM,**
148 Darlinghurst Road, Darlinghurst (9360 7999). A history of the Jewish people in Australia and the world.

☆ **JUSTICE AND POLICE MUSEUM,** corner of Phillip and Albert Streets, Circular Quay (9252 1144). It displays mug shots of Sydney crooks, the death mask of the bushranger Captain Moonlight, and relics of great crimes. Oddly, there's nothing about police corruption.

☆ **HARRIS STREET MOTOR MUSEUM,**
320 Harris Street, Pyrmont (9552 1210). Cars from the vintage to the futuristic.

☆ **SYDNEY TRAMWAY MUSEUM,** corner of Rawson Avenue and Pitt Streets, Loftus (9542 3646). It looks at the transport system we lost in 1961, and offers tram rides.

☆ **HALL OF CHAMPIONS,** in the Sports Centre, Australia Avenue, Homebush (9763 0111). Memorabilia of 40 sports, including Freddie Lane's 1900 gold medal.

☆ **MACLEAY AND NICHOLSON MUSEUMS,** University of Sydney, Parramatta Road, Camperdown (9692 2274). Wonderfully weird stuff including mummies, embalmed ibises and preserved lice from Captain Cook's ship.

64
kids

*t*here is no excuse for a kid to be bored in Sydney, provided a parent has time, energy and money. Apart from Sydney's 70 beaches, the museums and parks (see separate chapters), the following activities might fill the odd weekend or school holiday.

☆ **AMUSEMENT AREAS.** Darling Harbour (9286 0111) in the city centre offers much to climb and swing on, souvenir shops, cafes, a Chinese garden, a miniature train, and the world's biggest cinema screen—usually showing natural history programs—in the Imax Theatre (133 462). Adjoining it is Sega World with virtual reality rides and video games. Much further west at Eastern Creek, Australia's Wonderland (9830 9100) is a traditional fun park with wild rides, wildlife and an artificial beach.

☆ **ANIMALS.** Taronga Zoo (9969 2777) in Mosman has got the lot. Fairfield City Farm (9823 3222) at Abbotsbury has quieter creatures. Kindifarm (9970 8708) can come to you with a mobile nursery that offers bottle-feeding of lambs, kids and a calf, hand-feeding of sheep and goats, patting piglets, and nursing rabbits. Pony rides can be included.

☆ **AQUARIUMS.** Sydney Aquarium (9262 2300) at Darling Harbour includes a glass tunnel with sharks swimming overhead. Oceanworld (9949 2644) at Manly has seal shows.

☆ **NATURE.** The Coastal Environment Centre (9970 6905) at North Narrabeen offers canoe trips on Narrabeen Lagoon, wildlife workshops and field trips to Manly Dam. The Bicentennial Park (9763 1844) at Homebush Bay has 50 hectares of wetlands including a protected conservation area with a waterbird refuge, which can be viewed from the Wetlands Explorer Train.

☆ **QUAINTNESS.** Nutcote (9953 4453) at Neutral Bay was the home of the children's author May Gibbs, creator of Snugglepot and Cuddlepie, and now contains a tearoom, giftshop and displays about her life and the botanical accuracy of her work.

☆ **SPOOKINESS.** The heritage township in the old Quarantine Station (9977 6522) at Manly offers ghost tours by lantern with scary stories, tea and damper. There are also less scary daytime tours.

185

☆ **STARGAZING.** Sydney Observatory (9217 0485) at Observatory Hill near the Rocks, often hosts public nights for viewing the moon and planets and playing with gadgets.

☆ **SLEEPOVERS.** Stay overnight in a hammock the way the convicts did at Hyde Park Barracks (9223 8922) or sleep in a submarine at the National Maritime Museum in Darling Harbour (9552 7555).

☆ **PARTIES.** Themed parties are all the rage now with Sydney kids. Some organisers will come to your home: Bill Bell's Magic Circus (9153 6042) who specialises in old-time showmanship, using rabbits, birds and guinea pigs; Lulu's Mexican Parties (9502 4336) who'll paint your face and let you dance the macarena and spear the pinata; and Barbie Parties (9482 3328) who will make your home pink and frilly for hours. And there are some party places you must travel to: the Dinostore in Newtown (9557 4637) which constructs a party around dinosaur adventures; bread-baking parties at Demeter Organic Bakery in Glebe (9660 2555); plaster painting with pre-formed statuettes at Plaster Master in North Bondi (9130 4855) or at the Plaster Funhouse in North Turramurra (9449 2475); and fairy fun at Spot the Magic Dragon in Randwick (9399 8324).

☆ **INFO.** There is a free monthly magazine for parents called *Sydney's Child*, which claims a circulation of 86 000 (9484 5334).

65
the harbour

*a*rthur Phillip declared it 'the finest natural harbour in the world' and Sydney people know he's right. They're always on it, in yachts, motor cruisers, ferries and rowboats. Or around it, picnicking in one of the parks on its 240 kilometres of foreshore. It occupies an area of 55 square kilometres, from the Heads at the eastern end (near Watsons Bay) to where the Parramatta River spills into it at the western end (near Birchgrove).

To experience the harbour, the boatless need only head for Circular Quay and jump on a ferry. If you go on a Saturday or Sunday afternoon between September and March, you'll see the 18-footers racing, in a ritual that began in 1895 with boats that were then wooden planks but which are now aluminium and plastic technotoys—the fastest single-hulled yachts in the world. They zip across the calm water, watched by ferryloads of spectators who are placing not-quite-legal bets. The racers divide between two main factions: the Sydney Flying Squadron and the Australian 18-footers.

In the middle of the Harbour is an island called Fort Denison, nicknamed Pinchgut, apparently for its effect on the convicts who used to be left there on minimum rations as punishment. It was called Rock Island till 1857, when a martello tower was built to watch for invading ships. Its cannons have never been fired, but they can be examined during one of the daily tours conducted by the Sydney Harbour National Park Information Centre, which is at Cadman's Cottage, 110 George Street (9247 5033).

The Centre can also arrange visits to the park lands and historical sites on Shark Island, near Rose Bay (formerly an animal quarantine centre); Clark Island, near Darling Point (where Lieutenant Ralph Clark tried to start the colony's first vegetable garden in 1789); Rodd Island, near Birkenhead Point (a former biological research station); and Goat Island, near East Balmain (site of a convict quarry).

Since the 1980s, the Harbour's main role has shifted from work to pleasure as most of the trade shipping moved to Port Botany in Botany Bay (which is finally doing what the British Government intended it to do 200 years ago). The old industrial docks are being converted to tourist areas; Darling Harbour was first (a continuing project that started in 1984), followed by Walsh Bay. The old piers near Circular Quay are being turned into theatres, shopping complexes and housing, and the fingerwharf at Woolloomooloo will be a grand hotel. Ocean liners, which are essential to any great harbour, still tie up at Darling Harbour or at the passenger terminal near Circular Quay.

66
the Bridge

*W*hen you're driving over the Sydney Harbour Bridge, you are actually travelling on the Bradfield Highway. It's named after the person who persuaded the parliament of NSW in 1916 to order construction of a bridge across Port Jackson.

John Job Crew Bradfield had been the chief designing engineer for the NSW Public Works Department since 1891. Once the parliament made its decision, Bradfield supervised an international design competition for the bridge, chose the winning design and adapted it to his own taste (with art deco pylons that have no functional purpose). He fought off those who wanted to limit the bridge to cars and trams (while trains used a tunnel), arranged the demolition of 800 houses around the site, supervised the construction program from its start in 1926, and bore the mockery when the project took longer than expected (there was a version of the Lord's Prayer which went: 'Our 'arbour which art in Sydney, Good-o be thy name. Thy bridge be done, If not in '30 then in '31'). Then he swallowed the disappointment when it turned out not to be the world's longest single-span steel bridge, as he had hoped. Just as Sydney's bridge neared completion, New York opened its Bayonne Bridge, which was 63 centimetres longer than Sydney's 1149 metres. Bradfield had the consolation of knowing that, at a weight of 52 732 tonnes, it was (and remains) Australia's largest bridge.

To check it could do the job before the official opening, Bradfield had 96 railway engines driven onto the bridge—equivalent to the weight of 5900 cars, ten times as many as could actually fit. It sank by 16 millimetres, which Bradfield declared a satisfactory safety margin.

The first car to cross the bridge—on the Sunday before the opening ceremony—was a model-A Ford containing John Bradfield and his family. He deserved at least that.

At the opening ceremony on 19 March 1932, the Premier of NSW, Jack Lang, was preparing to snip the ribbon with golden scissors when a man on a horse rode through the crowd and slashed the ribbon with a sword. He turned out to be Francis de Groot, the owner of a furniture factory and a member of a right wing group called The New Guard, who objected to what they called Lang's socialist policies. The ribbon was tied back together, Lang snipped it, and de Groot was fined five pounds, plus four pounds costs, for offensive behaviour in a public place.

The NSW government finally paid off the bridge in 1988. Nowadays, the $2 toll charged for crossing it from north to south goes towards paying off a tunnel under the harbour which was built in 1992, and also towards bridge maintenance. It takes ten years and 30 000 litres of paint to apply one coat to the coathanger, and as soon as that's finished, the painting starts again.

The Sydney Harbour Bridge is now used by 150 000 vehicles every day but by surprisingly few pedestrians, considering that the middle of the walkway on its eastern side offers one of the finest viewing experiences in Sydney. There's also a bicycle path on the western side.

There are plans to run guided walking tours over the top of the arch, with the climbers connected by harnesses to a handrail (call Bridge Climb Sydney on 9252 0077 for details). At present, the less adventurous can climb up inside the southeast pylon, look at an exhibition on the building of the bridge, and still be knocked out by the view from the top.

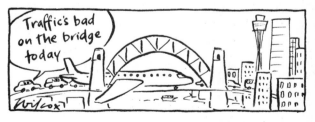

67
the Opera House

*t*he Opera House is the only Australian building known around the world. This would probably not be the case if it looked like a squat cylinder, or a flying saucer, or two giant shoeboxes. They were the runners-up in the international contest held in 1956 to design an opera house to sit on Bennelong Point in Sydney Harbour. Legend has it that when the 233 entries were first examined, the drawings by the Danish architect Joern Utzon weren't even shortlisted. They were spotted by accident in a pile of rejects by one of the judges, the American architect Eero Saarinen, who said to the others 'Gentlemen, this is your Opera House'.

When they announced the winner of the 5000 pound prize, the judges admitted that 'the drawings are simple to the point of being dramatic'. In the early 1960s, Utzon moved to Sydney to help with the many construction problems his simple drawings had left unsolved. The cost—intended to be covered by a state lottery—kept blowing out, and a new government elected in 1965 imposed limitations which Utzon couldn't tolerate. He resigned from the project in 1966, and the planning of the interior was left to local architects, Lionel Todd, David Littlemore and Peter Hall.

The Opera House finally opened in 1973 and cost $102 million ($95 million more than the original budget). Almost immediately it was criticised as being inadequate for grand opera—the opera theatre and the dressing rooms were too cramped.

The structure consists of three sets of overlapping shells that look like sails on the harbour but which Utzon said were based on orange segments. The tallest set of shells covers the concert hall, which seats 2680; the second set covers the opera theatre, which seats 1550; and the smallest shells cover the Bennelong restaurant. There's also a drama theatre (540) and a tiny playhouse (400). Utzon never returned to Sydney to see how his drawings turned out.

68
the skyline

*f*or the first half of this century, the authorities fought to stop Sydney becoming a high-rise city. While Manhattan and Chicago were soaring with temples of commerce, Sydney imposed a height limit of 150 feet (46 metres). Throughout the 1940s and 1950s, the tallest thing on the skyline was the white broadcasting tower on top of the AWA building in York Street, built in 1939. The rest of the office blocks were stumps of 12 storeys or less.

Australia's first serious skyscraper was the AMP insurance company's headquarters at Circular Quay, which was completed in 1962. Parliament had to pass a special act to allow AMP to build it, and it ended up twice as high as any other building of the time. Despite public scepticism and big problems with air conditioning, the AMP Building started a skyscraper boom, which picked up speed after 1965 with the election of Robert Askin's Liberal government. Askin believed in Progress and The Private Sector. He is supposed to have told his driver 'ride over the bastards' when confronted with some anti-Vietnam War protesters in the mid 1960s, and he took the same attitude to those who wanted to preserve historic buildings in the city centre. If the developers needed to build skyscrapers to hold the workers who would make money for Sydney, then the government's job was to clear away the obstacles.

The first building to reach 183 metres and soar higher than the Harbour Bridge was the Australia Square Tower on the corner of George and Hunter Streets, designed by Harry Seidler in 1967. Being round and white, it was a rare exception to the rectangular conformity of the time. The international fashion in high-rise design was 'less is more', which produced buildings that were elegantly austere at their best, and downright ugly when done on the cheap, as happened in Sydney through the 1970s. By 1980, the city centre was a clutter of big grey cornflakes packets. The blandness was marginally relieved by the construction in 1981 of the Centrepoint Tower (now called the Sydney Tower) which looks like a gold bucket on top of a stick (it's actually an observation dome on a lift shaft). At 304 metres, it remains the city's tallest structure, a monument to 70s kitsch.

But nowadays, if you stand on a vantage point—for example, the thin park at the north end of Victoria Street, Potts Point—and survey the Central Business District, you see a panorama of spectacularly varied tower tops. Something wonderful happened in the 1980s. Who'd have thought we'd ever be grateful for the vanity and extravagance of the 'greed is good' decade? Yet those were the forces responsible for the cavalcade of colourful new structures and reworked old structures that are, at their silliest, good for a giggle, and at their grandest, positively inspiring. They may be rich folks' follies, but they belong to us all now. Sydney—which missed out on most of the glories of the art deco period, and then got the worst of the 1960s boxiness—is becoming a paradise of postmodern parodies.

From the end of Victoria Street you can see what I call the Jules Verne Building because it looks like a blue snub-nosed rocket ship about to take a party of adventurers to the moon. It's actually 1 O'Connell Street, designed by the firm of Peddle Thorp and finished in 1991.

There's also the 1920s-looking Chifley Tower, originally commissioned in the mid 1980s by the entrepreneur Alan Bond and designed by the Chicago architects Kohn Pederson Fox. When Bond went broke, a Japanese firm bought the project, and the building was completed in 1993 at a total cost of more than a billion dollars. Looking back at us from the top of the Chifley Tower is Forty One, one of Sydney's finest restaurants.

The tallest block we can see from this eastern vantage point is the Governor Phillip Tower, 50 storeys and 223 metres above Phillip Street, which makes it five times the size of the tallest building in

We've produced loads of new paperwork to fill the unsightly holes around Sydney

1960. Its crown is called 'the gridiron' or 'the egg slicer'. It was designed by Richard Johnson of Denton Corker Marshall and finished in 1995. We'll go inside it in the next chapter.

If we head into town now, and stand on the corner of King and York Streets, it's possible to glimpse, on the surrounding corners, a few survivors of Sydney's brief flirtation with art deco. The best is the Grace Building, a scaled-down version of the Chicago Tribune Tower which was built as offices for Grace Bros department store in 1930. Its top is a modest gothic folly. The interior was restored in the mid 1990s to become a hotel, but it lacks the splendour you'd expect.

If we stand on the corner of George and Market Streets and look south (after enjoying the green domes and 19th century statuary around the roof of the Queen Victoria Building) we can contrast the 60s stolidity of the Hilton Hotel and the Electricity Commission buildings with the 80s frivolity of the Coopers & Lybrand building. Somehow Australia's biggest firm of accountants decided to move into a blue tower with a pink crown on top, like something from a 1950s comic strip (but actually built in 1990 from designs by Rice Daubney architects). I always expect to see Spider Man abseiling from its roof. It's been ridiculed, but it's proud to be postmodern.

If we head north now, towards the Rocks, we'll see the city's most stylish example of a recent

Sydney fad—converting working spaces into living spaces. The IBM building at 168 Kent Street used to be a dull office box, built in 1964. As the result of a conversion program by architects Crone and Associates from 1994 to 1996, it's now an apartment block, renamed The Observatory Tower. The architects added wrap-around verandahs to the facade, ten more floors, and a cute tower like a mortarboard on top. They painted it dark green and black because the client 'wanted it to be like a car— dark and slick and sexy and mysterious'.

Finally, let's head for the harbour foreshore and look across the water to McMahons Point, and the structure known as 'Sydney's most hated building'. Blues Point Tower was designed in 1960 by the argumentative Sydney architect, Harry Seidler. In the context of the cottages around it, it sticks out like a square thumb. It wasn't meant to. It was part of an elaborate scheme to cover the entire headland with 29 massive residential blocks, designed to thrust Sydney into an era of high-density, inner-city living. The scheme fell apart and Blues Point Tower was its only legacy. Should it be allowed to fall down? I don't think so. Now that the CBD is a showcase of curved facades, mirror glass, art deco references and eccentric rooftops, Blues Point Tower looks refreshingly simple. And it's a vivid reminder of a period when the whole city was square.

69
foyerism

*i*f you've come this far on the journey through this book, you'll be aware that Governors Arthur Phillip and Lachlan Macquarie loom large over the Sydney story. They are one reason why we are now standing in the lobby of the Governor Phillip Tower in Bridge Street, watching Arthur Phillip being swirled down the plughole of history. Well, that's what the tall metal sculpture by Rodney Broad looks like to me. It's called 'Willy Willy', so I suppose the vortex in which Phillip is spinning is meant to be a miniature tornado rather than water spiralling out of a bath.

In an adjoining foyer, a bronze Lachlan Macquarie in a high-buttoned jacket projects from the top of a metal pole like an orchid (or possibly a tall poppy), glaring at some massive paintings of the first European settlements in Sydney Cove. Sculptor Trevor Weekes clearly sees him as a stern and forceful leader, just as Rodney Broad apparently sees Phillip as the victim of nature.

The chance to see these pioneering figures is one reason to enter the adjoining lobbies of the Governor Phillip and Governor Macquarie Towers on the corner of Bridge and Phillip Streets. The other reason is that they are the most breathtaking modern foyers in the city. The angular entrance halls, which rise ten storeys, are like cathedrals.

In the spirit of the 1980s, when they were conceived, these foyers shout that the building owners have money to burn—or more accurately, space to spare. They are part of a new architectural spirit in Sydney, which says that lobbies are not just ways for workers to reach the lifts, but play spaces to awe and delight the whole populace.

The spirit is affecting both the new and the old—there's a craze for 'refacading' and 'relobbying' office blocks, a form of cosmetic surgery designed to give character to the bland boxes of the 1960s building boom. For anyone interested in art and design, the foyers of central Sydney are as attractive as the galleries and museums.

The Phillip and the Macquarie Towers were erected between 1992 and 1995 on the site of Sydney's first Government House, built for Arthur Phillip in 1788. Sculptures and paintings for the foyers were commissioned with this in mind. 'We wanted the art to interpret the fact of the site's history, and the briefings were given even before the building was there,' says Richard Johnson, project architect for the towers. 'It is a terribly important site, a very

Striking up a conversation in a lift. * 33

Was that you?

powerful site, and we know that the art had to be not just site-specific but that it also had to interpret the space in some way as well. Naturally, because of the historical nature of the site, it was important that we chose Australian artists.'

Just up the road is 1992's Chifley Tower (corner of Phillip and Loftus Streets) whose long marble lobby contains a huge Akio Makigawa sculpture and extravagant artworks by Colin Lanceley, Clifford Firth and Robert Jacks. The adjoining shopping and eating space is one of Sydney's liveliest people-watching areas.

Down on George Street near Circular Quay, Harry Seidler's Grosvenor Place (finished in 1988) has a lobby designed around three enormous Frank Stella creations that could be 3D paintings or multicoloured sculptures. Seidler deliberately kept the rest of the foyer stark to focus attention on the specially-commissioned artwork. He took a different approach to his 1990 Capita Centre, at 9 Castlereagh Street, turning the entryway into a forest of soaring trees (which is now where the office workers lurk to smoke).

But Sydney's modern architects were not the first to discover the power of a fine foyer. The early years of the 20th century were another golden age for lobbyists. On Martin Place, between Elizabeth and Castlereagh, squats the Commonwealth Savings Bank, built in beaux arts style in 1928 (mercifully just before the Depression struck). The main chamber, supported by Greek columns, was an attempt to awe the potential depositor with a sense of wealth and security. But continue to the back and you discover a magic staircase under a barrel-vaulted ceiling of mosaics, scrolls and stained glass scenes of happy toilers. Up the stairs (three floors of marbled magnificence), you peek into the managing director's inside garden at the bottom of a nine-storey glass atrium.

Still on Martin Place, just across Castlereagh Street, there's the art deco MLC building from 1936, now called the Minter Ellison building for the law firm that inhabits it. It offers the prettiest small foyer in town, with lamp sconces like icecream cones and multicoloured Egyptian columns. There was no such foyer in the original design—it was inserted during a renovation in 1988 to look like the sort of foyer they'd have created if they'd had the money in 1936. That's the new Sydney attitude for you—if history didn't provide a fabulous foyer, just go ahead and fake it.

70
graffiti

*t*he Sydney writer Richard Neville managed to annoy both neatness freaks and lesbians in mid 1997 when he remarked that 'a city without graffiti is like sex without sperm'. He was suggesting that the words of the prophets may very well be written on the subway walls, and that efforts to scrub off all public scribblings might diminish the spirit of Sydney. After all, he said, 'the only difference between graffiti and art is permission'.

The history of graffiti in the Sydney area goes back many thousands of years, in the form of 5500 sites where Aboriginal people carved or painted on the landscape (Sydney sandstone being ideally soft for that sort of thing). In the suburb of Allambie Heights, for example, there are 68 rock carvings in the Gumbooya Reserve. One carving seems to the European eye to be telling the story of Jonah and the Whale, which says something about the universality of myths. On the golf course at the northern end of Bondi Beach, the carvings include a small fish attacking a shark, which may be how the Eora people saw their relationship with their invaders.

The two prime areas to see rock art are the Royal National Park in the south (the original home of the

Tharawal people) and Ku-ring-gai Chase National Park in the north. The hundreds of engravings by the Ku-ring-gai people include fish, whales (some up to eight metres long), wallabies and mythical beings such as Daramulan, the father figure who created the land, the people and the animals. There are also cave paintings and hand stencils, done with ochre and charcoal, which are older than the pyramids of Egypt. The frequent images of men and women leaping for joy certainly predate the arrival of the Europeans.

The Europeans quickly made their own contribution to the rock galleries. Preserved under glass within the Garden Island naval base in Sydney Harbour is a rock on which are carved the initials FM, IB and WB, and the date 1788. FM has been identified as Frederick Meredith, who was steward to the captain of the First Fleet ship *Scarborough* and who was assigned to look after the vegetable patch on what was then an island. Perhaps we should add to Richard Neville's observation about graffiti and art that the only difference between vandalism and a tourist site is 200 years.

71
architects

*b*efore there were architects in Sydney there were convict builders, who threw the houses together so haphazardly that in 1794 the newly-arrived governor, John Hunter, feared there would be a mass collapse. He ordered the convicts to make lime from sea shells and plaster it all over the buildings to protect them against rain. The settlement in the early days must have looked like a Greek village.

Governor Lachlan Macquarie, who wanted to make Sydney a model of urban beauty, was relieved in 1814 by the arrival of a convict named Francis Greenway, sentenced to 14 years exile for forging a contract. Greenway was an experienced architect who had a letter of recommendation from the former governor, Arthur Phillip. Macquarie appointed him Acting Government Architect in 1816, and soon Greenway had prepared a plan for Sydney which, he said, would provide 'regular streets, upon the same principle as they are in London ... the most elegant, convenient and substantial buildings for every public accommodation to last for some centuries'.

Today, 11 of Greenway's 40 constructions are still standing, including Hyde Park Barracks in

Macquarie Street, St James Church in King Street, the Supreme Court building in Elizabeth Street, and St Matthews Church in Windsor.

Some of the other great contributors to the way Sydney looks include:

☆ **JAMES BARNET.** A Scottish builder who reached Sydney in 1854, he was Colonial Architect from 1862 to 1890, responsible for 1000 buildings, including the city's most magnificent Victoriana: the Australian Museum in College Street, the General Post Office in Martin Place, the Customs House at Circular Quay, the Colonial Secretary's Office on Macquarie and Bridge Streets, and the Lands Department on Bridge and Loftus Streets.

☆ **EDMUND BLACKET.** He built Sydney University in gothic style in the 1850s, then became the major architect of big buildings in the late 19th century, specialising in conservative-looking churches such as St Andrews Cathedral in the mid city, St Johns in Darlinghurst, and St Marks in Darling Point.

☆ **PHILIP COX.** Sydney's most successful designer of public buildings in the 1990s, he created the giant doughnut-shaped Sydney Football Stadium, the Sydney Harbour Casino, most of the structures around Darling Harbour, and the structures at Homebush for the Olympics.

☆ **BRUCE DELLITT.** In 1929, aged 29, he outraged conservative architects by using experimental art deco styles to win the design contest for the Anzac War Memorial in Hyde Park. He went on to create AFT House in O'Connell Street, one of Sydney's few surviving sculpted deco skyscrapers.

☆ **WALTER BURLEY GRIFFIN.** A disciple of Frank Lloyd Wright in Chicago, he won the contest for the design of Canberra in 1912, resigned in 1920, and went on to design (with his wife Marion) and develop the northern Sydney suburb of Castlecrag.

☆ **GLENN MURCUTT.** During the 1970s, he turned the tin shed into an art form, designing homes and restaurants to fit with Australian bush traditions and to make best use of light and air. His best-known work is Berowra Waters Inn (1977) and houses at Lot 1, Halcrows Road, Glenorie (1982) and 28 Hopetoun Avenue, Balmoral (1992).

☆ **HARRY SEIDLER.** Born in Vienna, he came to Australia in 1949 to design a house for his parents, and stayed to build a string of lean skyscrapers and to fight for the austere style called modernism. He's best known for the Blues Point Tower at McMahons Point, the Australia Square Tower in George Street, the MLC Centre on Martin Place, and Grosvenor Place near Circular Quay.

☆ **EMIL SODERSTEIN.** He started his own firm in 1925 when he was 24, and soon became, with Bruce Dellitt, the pioneer of art deco in Sydney, designing a variety of cinemas, the Canberra War Memorial, Birtley Towers in Elizabeth Bay, and the City Mutual building on the corner of Hunter and Bligh Streets.

☆ **ARTHUR STEPHENSON.** The firm he started in the 1930s, Stephenson and Turner, became Australia's biggest design practice, responsible for the art deco King George V Hospital in Camperdown and the slimline Sydney Dental Hospital in Elizabeth Street, Surry Hills.

☆ **JOHN SULMAN.** His finest building was the Thomas Walker Convalescent Hospital (1889) within Concord Hospital but he's best remembered for teaching architecture between 1910 and 1930 and endowing the Sir John Sulman Medal for Architecture.

☆ **WALTER VERNON.** Government architect from 1890 to 1911, he used an 'arts and crafts' decorative style in such designs as the Central Railway Station, the fire stations at Darlinghurst, Glebe and Pyrmont, the State Library of NSW, and the Art Gallery of NSW.

☆ **LESLIE WILKINSON.** He was Sydney University's first professor of architecture (serving from 1918 till 1947), designer of many of the university's 20th century buildings, and a fashionable designer of Mediterranean-style houses and flats in the 1930s. He named the Wilkinson Medal for Domestic Architecture.

72
stately homes

*a*s soon as Sydney started to get wealthy settlers, it started to get mansions whereby they
could show off their wealth. Here, in chronological
order, is a sampling of the ones still worth visiting.

☆ **ELIZABETH FARM,** 70 Alice Street,
Parramatta. Built by convicts for John
Macarthur in 1793, and somewhat remodelled
during the 18th century, this four-room brick
cottage is usually described as the oldest private
home in Australia.

☆ **EXPERIMENT FARM COTTAGE,** 9 Ruse
Street, Parramatta. Built in the late 1790s on
the site of James Ruse's first attempts to grow
wheat, it's a good place to see very early
colonial furniture.

☆ **OLD GOVERNMENT HOUSE,** O'Connell
Street, Parramatta. The oldest surviving public
building in Australia, it was built between 1799
and 1815 and was home to the colony's
governors until the 1850s.

☆ **ELIZABETH BAY HOUSE,** 7 Onslow Avenue,
Elizabeth Bay. Hailed as 'the finest house in the
colony' when it was built by fashionable
architect John Verge in 1839, it has an

extraordinary domed spiral staircase.

☆ **VAUCLUSE HOUSE,** Wentworth Road,
Vaucluse. A gothic Tudor mansion built during
the 1830s, it was for 20 years the home of the
political pioneer William Charles Wentworth.

☆ **ROSE SEIDLER HOUSE,** 71 Clissold Road,
Wahroonga. Built in 1950 by the architect
Harry Seidler for his parents, it's now a
monument to modernist minimalism, filled with
original 1950s experimental furniture.

73
streets

*t*he most common street name in Sydney is
Park—there are 114 of them. But none of the
Park Streets is as interesting as these for a full-day
stroll:

☆ **APPIAN WAY,** Burwood. The whole street was
created between 1903 and 1911 by an
entrepreneur named George Hoskins, to be 'an
ideal suburban environment for the Sydney of
the new century'. It's the country's best
collection of the design style called Federation
Architecture, with lots of trees, a recreation area
including a croquet lawn, and gracious cottages
and mansions on extensive grounds. Each home
is individually named—Colonna, Atela, Capri,
Ravenna, Toscana, Verona, Lavinia, etc.

☆ **KING STREET,** Newtown. In the process of
trendification, it still offers a glorious hodge-
podge of cheap restaurants and cafes, feral
clothing and furniture shops, delis, bookshops
(notably Gould's at 519), record stores, and
gay or lesbian pubs.

☆ **MACQUARIE STREET,** in the city. It's
Sydney's most historic avenue, laid out by the
governor himself. Starting at the Opera House

end, these are my favourite structures to gawp at and sneak into: Government House on the left, a mock-gothic castle built in 1845 and occupied by vice-regal personages till 1996; the absurd Government House stables, actually built before the main mansion and now the Conservatorium of Music; then on the right, the Ritz-Carlton Hotel, in Sydney's old venereal disease clinic; the Intercontinental Hotel, an ugly tower inside the elegant old sandstone Treasury Building from 1896; the Colonial Secretary's Office from 1875; the Astor apartments from the decadent 1920s; and BMA House, an art deco masterpiece from 1930, topped with armoured gargoyles. Now the action moves to the left side again, with the Greek-revival State Library built in stages between 1905 and 1935, and a glassy new wing built in 1988; Parliament House, built originally in 1812 as part of the Rum Hospital, but turned over to the politicians in 1829; Sydney Hospital, built in 1894 with a bronze boar outside giving good luck if you rub his nose (and just inside the grounds there's a little oasis, containing an eccentric black and yellow fountain with green flamingoes and black swans); the old Mint, also built as part of the Rum Hospital in 1816 but converted for coin making in 1854; and the Hyde Park Barracks, designed by Francis Greenway, built to house convicts in 1819 and now a museum (a dormitory with hammocks has been reconstructed on the third floor).

☆ **OXFORD STREET,** from Darlinghurst to Woollahra. Beginning with the pubs and cafes of Sydney's gay area (known as The Pink Precinct), Oxford Street passes two of Sydney's best cinema arthouses, the Verona and the Academy Twin, and two of Sydney's best bookshops, Ariel and Berkeleouw's. As it enters Paddington, it passes the Victoria Barracks on the right, still as they were in 1848, and then Juniper Hall on the left, restored to its 1824 glory. From there it offers three blocks of the best fashion shopping in the suburbs and the best French restaurant in Sydney (Claude's). Before it fizzles out in Bondi Junction, it offers the restful spaces of Centennial Park.

74
parks

*b*y now you won't be surprised to learn that Sydney's first park was laid out and fenced in by Governor Lachlan Macquarie in 1810. It was **Hyde Park**. It contained a racecourse until 1821, and a cricket ground until 1856. Nowadays, it's a 17 hectare refreshment zone for city workers and a snogging zone for lovers, with a monument at either end. To the north, there's the fountain of Greek myths designed by the French sculptor Francois Sicard in 1932 and funded by the *Bulletin* editor Jules Archibald. To the south, there's the massive art deco war memorial which won Bruce Dellitt a design competition in 1929.

Sydney's second public park was also Macquarie's work—an area called the Government Domain which was fenced off in 1810 and opened to respectable citizens in 1816 when a road was put through to a rocky outcrop later called Mrs Macquarie's Chair. The area, which included the site of the colony's first farm, came to be the **Royal Botanic Gardens**. Now it covers 29 hectares and includes a cactus garden, a herb garden, palm groves and a pyramid-shaped glasshouse.

And when we come to Sydney's largest park, we

still can't escape the Governor. In 1811, he set aside an area four kilometres east of the city to be part of the water supply. It came to be known as Lachlan Swamps, and water was pumped into town from its ponds until 1859. In 1888, to commemorate the centenary of European arrival, it was officially dedicated 'to the enjoyment of the people of NSW for ever'. On 1 January 1900, 100 000 people gathered in **Centennial Park** to watch the ceremony which united six colonies into a nation called Australia. Nowadays, its 220 hectares are visited by three million people a year, picnicking, feeding the ducks, riding horses, using the cycling and roller blading tracks, jogging, barbecuing, and eating in the kiosk.

A hundred years after the opening of Centennial Park, a similarly ambitious project began to the west of the city—**Bicentennial Park** on Homebush Bay. It includes 50 hectares of mangrove swamps, through which pass raised boardwalks, and an ornamental lake, cycling tracks, forests, a teahouse and views of the site for the year 2000 Olympics.

The other big recreation space close to the city centre (11 kms northwest of the Bridge) stretches along a river cruised by ducks and a paddle-wheeler. The **Lane Cove National Park**, is more like 31 picnic grounds in search of a wilderness.

215

ICONS

75
beaches

*M*ost Sydney beaches are (a) not as polluted as they used to be, following improvements to the treatment methods at Manly, Bondi and Malabar sewerage outlets; (b) safe from sharks, since netting was introduced in the 1930s; (c) comfortable about women going topless; and (d) skin cancer traps, so protect yourself by using a 15-plus sunscreen and not lying around between 11am and 2pm.

So with 70 beaches strung along the edge of the city and around the Harbour, there's plenty of choice for every taste.

☆ **BOARDRIDING.** The best are said to be North Narrabeen in the north and Maroubra in the south, but they get crowded and the local riders are unfriendly to strangers. Almost as good are Queenscliff (north end of Manly), Wanda (way down south) and Palm Beach (way up north), especially for new riders.

☆ **FAMILY SWIMMING.** Nielsen Park at Vaucluse has big trees for picnicking under, a kiosk with good espresso, and a beach that's more like a pool. Bronte Beach has a protected children's swimming area, a long bushy park

with a playground, and terrific cafes across the road. Coogee is so sheltered that it rarely gets big waves, and there are cliffs at both ends for kite flying or strolling, plus the magnificent Wylie's Baths a short walk to the south. Shelley Beach, just south of Manly's surf beach, has rockpools, shady spots and picnic areas.
Balmoral Beach has a genteel 1920s atmosphere and one of Sydney's best restaurants—the Bathers Pavilion—with a casual cafe attached if you want to stay in your togs.

☆ **HISTORY.** Camp Cove, just inside the entrance to Sydney Harbour near Watsons Bay, was where Captain Phillip first landed on 20 January 1788, after he set off from Botany Bay to find a better place to found a colony. Freshwater Beach at Harbord was the site of Australia's first surfboard riding demonstration, by the Hawaiian Olympic swimming champion Duke Kahanamoku in 1915 (the plank he used is still visible in the Freshwater lifesaving clubhouse). Coogee Beach was the place where, in 1922, Frank Beaurepaire won a bravery award of 2500 pounds for trying to rescue a shark attack victim. He used the money to start the Olympic tyre company.

217

☆ **NUDISM.** The most
accessible nudist beach is Lady Bay, also
known as Lady Jane, which is at Watsons Bay,
just round from Camp Cove. There's also Reef
Beach, a long walk round the shoreline from
Manly's harbour side, and Cobbler's Beach,
east of Balmoral Beach but best accessed by
boat.

☆ **STARSPOTTING.** Palm Beach is for the
millionaires, Whale Beach (far north) is for the
actors who don't want to be recognised, and
Tamarama (next to Bondi, and also known as
Glamarama) is for the show-offs. The Bondi
area is a film-makers' colony, but they'd rather
drink coffee than swim.

76
Bondi

*b*ondi was officially named in 1827, from an Aboriginal word which apparently meant 'the noise of water breaking on rocks'. The beach was privately owned until 1856 when the newly-formed colonial parliament had the sense to acquire it as an asset for use by every citizen. Now it's Australia's most legendary beach.

Bondi became a resort for daytrippers in the 1890s, especially after the tram started running in 1894, and in the early 1900s it was the scene of campaigns designed to have daytime surf bathing legalised. As soon as that happened, the world's first surf lifesaving club was formed there in February 1906.

The first captain of the club, Lyster Ormsby, is credited with inventing the lifesaving reel—hemp rope was wound around a giant cotton reel and life-savers could carry a belt at the end of the rope out to swimmers in trouble and then be towed back to shore. One of the first official rescues at Bondi was a kid named Charlie Smith from North Sydney, who was pulled to safety on 3 January 1907. He later became the aviation pioneer Sir Charles Kingsford Smith.

The current look of Bondi comes from the 1930s, when lots of hotels and apartment blocks were built in a style best described as 'cheapo deco'. The surf pavilion, the walkways and the little bridges were built during the Depression as part of employment relief programs. The oceanfront has been subject to regular 'improvement' schemes ever since, designed to reduce traffic problems. But there's just no stopping people from visiting an asset like this, just 7 km from the centre of town, and Campbell Parade is now an intense concentration of cafes, surf shops, bars and fast food outlets.

Despite the overdevelopment, Bondi remains one of the great places to surf. It also offers—for the less energetic—a bracing cliff walk at its southern end.

77
Manly

*W*hile Bondi gets the publicity, Manly can boast a far more interesting history. It was named in 1788 by Governor Phillip, who took a look at the local Aboriginal people and wrote: 'Their confidence and manly bearing made me give the name of Manly Cove to this place'. Phillip was later speared by one of the locals, but left the punishing of the culprit to Bennelong, his 'ambassador' to the Eora people.

Manly didn't get going as a village until the 1850s when an entrepreneur named Henry Smith started a ferry service between it and Sydney Cove, and built a road from the Harbour landing spot to the ocean beach. He called the road The Corso, after a street he liked in Rome, and he lined it with refreshment tents, mazes, swings and gardens. Manly was a holiday resort 50 years before Bondi.

Manly's biggest moment happened on 1 October 1902 when a local newspaper editor named William Gocher decided to challenge a law that had been passed in 1838 banning public swimming between 6am and 8pm. He went into the water at midday (in a neck-to-knee costume) but the police were so reluctant to act that he had to go in twice more before they would arrest him. The local council became a laughing stock and in 1903 the law was rescinded, creating a precedent for surfers all across Sydney. Manly beach continued to lead the way— the world's first swimming carnival was held there in 1908 and the first official surfboard riding championship in 1964.

Manly is still one of Sydney's best surfing beaches, with Shelley Beach, just round the corner, providing an ideal spot for toddlers to get used to the water. The suburb round The Corso retains a resort atmosphere that almost lives up to the slogan of the old Manly ferries: 'Seven miles from Sydney and a thousand miles from care'.

78
wildlife

O f the three creatures chosen as Sydney's mascots for the 2000 Olympics—Millie the echidna, Syd the platypus and Olly the kookaburra—only the kookaburra is likely to be experienced by any visitor to the city. Its laughter (which it uses to claim its territory) can be heard in Sydney's northern suburbs as it sits on trees or powerlines.

Birds have long been Sydney's most noteworthy wildlife. In a diary entry for 26 January 1788, a First Fleet naval officer named Arthur Smyth noted that 'the singing of the various birds among the trees, and the flight of the numerous parraquets, lorrequets, cockatoos and maccaws, made all around appear like an enchantment'. He probably mistook a parrot for a macaw—they are not among the 370 species of birds native to Australia, although they have been introduced in the past 200 years along with about 400 other foreign species.

The budgerigar, which is the world's most popular caged bird, was native to Sydney and was taken to Europe for breeding in the 1830s. These days the most commonly-seen birds around town are the magpie (watch out for their swooping attacks during springtime), the willie wagtail, the magpie lark, the welcome swallow, the black-faced cuckoo shrike, the galah, the sulphur-crested cockatoo, the rainbow lorikeet, and the common starling. During the 1990s, the parks of inner Sydney have been overrun by a plague of ibises.

There's a colony of bats—more precisely grey-headed flying foxes—in the northern suburbs near Gordon, and it's a Sydney summer ritual to watch them flying across the harbour at sunset, heading for the fig trees in the Botanic Gardens, Moore Park and Centennial Park, where they hang upside-down and munch all night.

Sydney has a long-nosed bandicoot colony on North Head, which is threatened by development plans, and a colony of squirrel gliders in the Barrenjoey Peninsula area, also endangered by human invasion.

There is, however, no shortage of ring-tail and brush-tail possums, which are famous for leaping

onto suburban roofs at night and for eating out of the hands of walkers in Hyde Park.

As for koalas and kangaroos—the best way to get close to them in Sydney is to visit Taronga Zoo.

79
dangers

Sydney has the most poisonous spider in the world, but don't panic. There are plenty of other menaces to take your mind off the funnel-webs. For example . . .

☆ **SHARKS.** The east coast of Australia has recorded more than 200 shark attacks this century. Sydney's beaches have been much safer since netting was introduced in 1937, but sharks sometimes congregate in Sydney Harbour to breed, and there have been a couple of incidents in recent years of swimmers being nipped in the Harbour or the adjoining rivers. The most dangerous sharks are the great white, the tiger and the bullshark.

☆ **BLUE-RINGED OCTOPUS.** It's about 20 cm long and a dull brown until it gets angry, when it takes on a bluish glow. Each one contains enough neurotoxin to kill ten adults. There is no antidote, and if you're stung, you must go to hospital and be put on life support until the effects wear off. The good news is that there have been only two deaths from blue-ringed octopi this century.

☆ **BLUEBOTTLES.** Each year some 10 000

beach swimmers in Australia are stung by bluebottles, also called the Portuguese man of war. It's not actually a jellyfish but a hydrozoan, which is a bluish bubble with no brain, no heart and no circulatory system but a trailing string that sticks venomous barbs into you if you brush against it. It's agonising but not fatal; you'll get red weals which will fade after a couple of days. Vinegar is the traditional remedy. Rubbing sand into the sting only makes it worse.

☆ **SNAKES.** The most dangerous around Sydney are death adders, which grow up to one metre and lie half-buried in soil or litter; the eastern brown snake, which grows up to 1.5 m; the eastern mainland tiger snake (up to 1.2 m); the red-bellied black snake (1.5 m); and the Sydney broad-headed snake (1.5 m). Each year the eastern brown and the tiger snake bite, on average, 100 Australians, of whom two die because they don't get antivenom in time.

☆ **SPIDERS.** The most deadly is the funnelweb, which lives in holes in the ground, mostly in Sydney's northern suburbs. It is black and heavily built and can be up to 8 cm long. About ten people a year get bitten, but there have been no deaths recently, thanks to antivenom. Next is the eastern mouse spider, which also lives in the ground. Its bite is most likely to affect children—in the early 1990s, one girl went into a coma for 12 hours after a bite but survived. It has a blackish body about 3 cm long, long jaws, and a grey or blue mark on the abdomen. Next comes the redback, small, with a red spot on a dark back. It lives in leaves or litter, and bites about 100 people a year, who get treated with antivenom. And finally there's the white-tail spider, with a cylindrical dark grey body and a white-tipped tail. The bacteria on its fangs can cause necrosis—rotting of the flesh—and there is no antidote. If in doubt, squash.

80
rats

*a*ustralia's native rodents were no match for the little terrors that ran eagerly off the ships that docked at Botany Bay and Sydney Cove in 1788. By 1900 they were so prolific that they caused an outbreak of bubonic plague in the Rocks area of Sydney—an epidemic that was encouraged by the filthy conditions of the inner city. There was a massive clean-up program and thousands of rats were destroyed after 303 people were confirmed as having the disease. More than 100 of them died in the first seven months of the outbreak.

The bright side was that the chief medical officer of NSW, Dr J Ashburton Thompson, made a world research breakthrough, proving that bubonic plague is caused by a bacterium, *Yersinia pestis*, which is transmitted to humans by fleas from infected rats.

The plague was declared eradicated from Australia in 1906 but the rats haven't gone away. The Sydney City Council produces regular maps of 'rodent activity' in the inner city. I doubt if ratwatching by night will become Sydney's hot new tourist attraction, but if you should wish to participate in this activity, the top spots are the Rocks, just around from Circular Quay; behind Wynyard railway station; the Haymarket; Martin Place near Castlereagh Street; the north and south ends of Hyde Park; in front of St Mary's Cathedral; and Macquarie Street, opposite Government House.

81
hospitals

Sydney's first hospital was a collection of tents set up in 1790 to look after the sick and injured from the horrific journey of the Second Fleet. It grew into a set of flimsy structures at Dawes Point, but the conditions there appalled Governor Macquarie when he arrived in 1809. Without permission from the British Government, he set about building a permanent hospital in Macquarie Street. He gave the building contractors a monopoly on the importation of rum for three years, plus 20 convicts to work for them, 20 bullocks, and 80 oxen whose meat they were allowed to sell. His wife helped design the structure, which was completed in 1816 without the government needing to pay a penny. The north wing of the Rum Hospital became Australia's first parliament house in 1829 and the south wing became the Sydney Mint in the 1850s. The central block was demolished in 1879 and what is now Sydney Hospital rose from its rubble.

Treatment for urgent cases in the public wards of Australian hospitals is free, while patients who want their own specialist doctors or private accommodation pay fees.

Sydney's major hospitals include:

- ☆ Centre for Bone and Joint Diseases, North Ryde
- ☆ Concord: Olympics-related problems
- ☆ Hornsby Kur-ing-gai: geriatric
- ☆ King George V, Camperdown: obstetrics and gynaecology
- ☆ New Children's, Westmead
- ☆ Prince Henry, Little Bay: infectious diseases
- ☆ Prince of Wales, Randwick: teaching and research, prison health
- ☆ Royal Hospital for Women (attached to Prince of Wales): cancers, obstetrics and gynaecology
- ☆ Royal North Shore, St Leonards: spinal injury, acute care in brain injury
- ☆ Royal Prince Alfred, Camperdown: teaching and research, cancer, world's biggest melanoma unit
- ☆ Royal Rehabilitation Centre, Ryde: state centre for spinal and brain injury
- ☆ St George, Kogarah: general care
- ☆ St Vincents, Darlinghurst: heart, AIDS, breast cancer (Garvan Institute), cancer
- ☆ Sydney, Macquarie Street: occupational health, hands, eyes
- ☆ Sydney Children's (attached to Prince of Wales)
- ☆ Westmead: kidney and pancreas transplants, foetal and neo-natal, HIV research, and a special health service for homeless, disturbed or disadvantaged young people.

82
schools

*t*he first school in Sydney was run by two convicts, Isabella and William Richardson, who taught mainly religious lessons in a church building from 1790 until 1810 when they returned to London. Later, William Richardson boasted that in all his time in Sydney, he had never been across the harbour to the north shore and had never bothered to travel the 20 kilometres to Parramatta—a very modern Sydney attitude.

Nowadays, there are about 900 government-run schools in Sydney and about 350 private schools (two-thirds of them run by the Catholic Church). Attendance is compulsory from the ages of six to 15. At the end of year 10 (the fourth year of high school) students receive the School Certificate, judged partly by assessment and partly by an exam. At the end of year 12 (the sixth and final year of high school), they receive the Higher School Certificate, judged mainly by an exam, and those results are used to assess their suitability for entrance into university and other tertiary courses.

In recent years, broad patterns suggest that in the HSC, single sex schools (particularly girls schools) have performed much better than co-educational schools, Catholic schools have performed better than government schools, and students living on the north shore and in the eastern suburbs get higher scores than students living in the outer western suburbs.

The government system offers places in what are called selective high schools to students seen as smarter than the average—there are 16 of these schools in Sydney. The NSW Teachers Federation says the selective system concentrates resources in a few schools and lowers general standards.

The schools which obtained the best results in the 1996 HSC were James Ruse Agricultural (co-ed selective), Fort Street (co-ed selective), North Sydney Girls (selective), Sydney Girls (selective), St George Girls (selective), Moriah College (Jewish private), Kambala (Anglican girls), Abbotsleigh (Anglican girls), Ascham (private girls) and Sydney Grammar (Anglican boys).

Sydney's most expensive private schools are Kings (founded in 1832 by the Church of England for boys), Sydney Grammar (Anglican boys), Ascham (a non-religious school for girls), Scots College (Anglican boys), Cranbrook (Anglican boys) and Abbotsleigh (Anglican girls). The size of the fees does not necessarily correlate with the size of the HSC score.

This year's education policy sees the return of the three 'R's: Revision, Regression and Regurgitation.

Wilcox

83
universities

*t*he university of Sydney was founded in 1852 with three lecturers imported from Britain and 24 students, only three of whom stayed to complete their degrees five years later. These days, Sydney University is Australia's biggest with 30 000 students. Its strengths are said to be medicine, veterinary science, law and the humanities. Australia's first chair of Australian Literature was established there in 1962.

There are now four other universities in Sydney:

☆ **THE UNIVERSITY OF NSW.** Founded in 1948 and now with 27 000 students, it is well regarded for science, business and economics.

☆ **MACQUARIE UNIVERSITY.** Begun in 1964, now with 17 000 students, it has a reputation for computing, teaching and social sciences.

☆ **THE UNIVERSITY OF TECHNOLOGY.** Established in 1988 from the NSW Institute of Technology, it has 21 000 students and is preferred for journalism, commerce and engineering.

☆ **THE UNIVERSITY OF WESTERN SYDNEY.** Founded in 1989 and now with 23 000 students, it scores for job-oriented courses in areas such as agriculture, technology and business.

Dr Stephen Matchett, a marketing consultant, provided this profile of their competing images:

'*University of Sydney*: High prestige vehicle of ancient lineage. All old oak and leather but there is a perception in the trade that perhaps the quality control team has not been spending as much time on the assembly line as they should. However, a vehicle with such an enormous brand loyalty that any engineering problem can definitely be fixed.

UNSW: The high-tech performer. A vehicle with all the bells and whistles, with a justly-earned reputation as the car of choice for the intellectual high achievers.

Macquarie: A reliable, family four-wheel-drive without the status of the Sydney or the glitz of the UNSW marque. The Macquarie will get you from A to B in comfort and provides value for money.

University of Technology: The specialist sports model of the Macquarie, pitching itself to a couple of specialist markets. Despite its youth, it is already commanding brand loyalty.

University of Western Sydney: The people's car. Caters for the mass market and is proud to do so. Without the sophisticated styling of some of the older marques, it is, however, a reliable vehicle with better performance than some writers expect.'

235

84
the inner west

*t*he inner western suburbs are academia shading into ethnicity, with a bit of bohemia on the side. Glebe, being next to Sydney's oldest university, has a scholarly air. The cafes of Glebe Point Road are the part of Sydney where you are most likely to overhear a discussion about philosophy or literature. (By comparison, the topic would be low-budget films in the cafes of Darlinghurst Road, and gardening or nannies in Military Road, Mosman).

Moving westwards, Glebe's terraces and row houses give way to the grander homes of Annandale and then to the semi-detached houses of Leichhardt, where many Italian immigrants settled in the 1950s and 1960s. North of Leichhardt is Balmain, branded a suburb of 'basketweavers' by the former Prime Minister Paul Keating, because of its left-wing politics. It's one of Sydney's oldest working class areas, settled by sailors and boatbuilders in the 1840s, now thoroughly gentrified.

On the southern side of Sydney University there's Newtown, an impoverished immigrant area until the 1970s, now mainly a mix of gays, lesbians, ferals, hippies, upwardly mobile young families, and students.

The key streets in the inner west are Glebe Point Road, with bookshops, restaurants, the Valhalla Cinema and, at the water end, the corrugated iron artists' studios (incorporating the Black Wattle Canteen); Norton Street, Leichhardt, with Italian restaurants and food stores; Darling Street, Balmain, with antique stores, cafes, and New Age arcana; and King Street, Newtown, with cafes, delis, gay and lesbian pubs, and grunge furniture and clothing shops.

The best part of the inner west for a Sunday stroll is Balmain, between Darling Street and Sydney Harbour, past sandstone cottages, terraces, mansions, churches and pubs built between 1840 and 1890. If you walk as far as Louisa Road, Birchgrove, you'll get fine harbour views and the chance of glimpsing Judy Davis.

85

the inner east

*t*he inner eastern suburbs are bohemia shading into yuppieville, or sleaze shading into success. At one extreme, there's Kings Cross (aka The Cross), a 24-hour-a-day parade of sex shops, prostitutes, strip clubs and shooting galleries (for heroin users). At the other extreme, there's Paddington (aka Paddo), a parade of antique shops, restaurants, fashion stores and art galleries (for credit card users).

In between, there's Woolloomooloo (aka The 'Loo), an inspiring reconstruction of a rundown suburb to provide public housing; Potts Point, where the giant terraces are either backpackers' hostels or rich folks' mansions; Elizabeth Bay, a treat for lovers of art deco architecture and Harbour glimpses; and Darlinghurst (aka Darlo), home of gays, artists and would-be filmmakers—the caffeine capital, the pink precinct, the land of the midnight sunglasses. This diversity is concentrated in an area of less than 8 square kilometres where often the extremes co-exist within the one block.

The key streets in the inner east are Oxford Street, with gay pubs, bookshops, restaurants, arthouse cinemas and clothing shops; and Victoria Street, Darlinghurst, between William and Burton Streets, with an intense concentration of cafes (most with good coffee, some with acceptable food).

The best place for a Sunday stroll is Paddington, a suburb developed for workers' housing in the 1880s, a slum by the 1940s, and a renovator's delight in the 1970s. The oldest terrace houses (1850s) are in Prospect Street, and the most beautiful terraces are in Ormond, Paddington and Hargrave Streets.

But be careful of small brown lumps on the footpath. The dog walkers of Paddo are less careful than they should be about picking up their pets' deposits. In the mid 1990s a mysterious person started placing tiny Australian flags in the poo piles of Paddo, trying to create either a patriotic statement or a set of new tourist sites.

Wed. May 15: Doug the dungbeetle becomes the first to climb the tallest mountain in Paddington, in the name of his country.

86
the north shore

*t*he greatest divide in Sydney is not between races or classes or religions. It's between the north shore and The Rest. The Rest are convinced that the North contains a bunch of snobs who vote Liberal, favour the monarchy, drink tea (while The Rest drink coffee), send their kids to private schools, go to Anglican churches (at Christmas and Easter), employ gardeners, and live in huge houses they inherited rather than worked for. The north shore only crosses the Bridge to visit the office and attend the Opera. The Rest would only cross the Bridge to commit a burglary.

As with most stereotypes, there's a little truth there. The area between the office blocks of North Sydney and the foliage of Wahroonga does tend to elect conservative MPs to parliament. Within the Liberal Party, the strip from Lindfield to Turramurra is called 'the Bible Belt'. And there are sumptuous gardens in suburbs such as Pymble, Gordon and Waitara. The houses tend to have many bedrooms and two-car garages.

Few of the top-rating restaurants in the annual *Good Food Guide* are north of the Bridge, but then, the North has Taronga Zoo, Tokyo Mart, Balmoral

Beach, the Wildflower Garden at St Ives, the bat colony at Gordon and an amazing gothic sandstone bridge between Cammeray and Northbridge (built by property developers in 1889 to boost sales on the northern side).

The spine of the north shore is the Pacific Highway, which has lively offshoots at North Sydney (Miller Street) and Crows Nest (Willoughby Road for restaurants and the Constant Reader bookshop). The most interesting thoroughfare is Military Road, with Neutral Bay's buzzing bars and cafes at one end and Mosman's fashion stores at the other.

The best place for a Sunday stroll is Castlecrag, a suburb designed in the 1920s by Walter Burley Griffin (who also designed Canberra). On a steep hill overlooking Sailors Bay, he built spiralling streets with names such as the Bulwark, the Scarp, the Battlement and the Rampart, and nestled sandstone cottages into the leafy environment. He banned fences, so that the housing would look cooperative, not competitive, because he felt that egotism was to blame for much of the environmental damage caused by other forms of building. Whether the north shore has achieved his goal and managed to transcend the ego is a question we'd better not put to The Rest of Sydney.

87
the other Sydney

*W*hen Governor Phillip discovered fertile land at the head of the Parramatta River in April 1788, he declared that he would have founded the colony on this spot if he'd known about it earlier. 'It was the best land I have seen in this country, and as fine as I have seen in England,' he wrote, and set about establishing farms there.

The township he called Rose Hill, 23 kilometres west of Sydney, expanded rapidly. By 1792 it had 2000 citizens while a mere 1200 lived at Sydney Cove, which was regarded simply as 'a depot for stores'. James Ruse proved he could become self-sufficient in wheat farming at Rose Hill in 1790, and John Macarthur made it the site of his sheep breeding experiments from 1793. In the early 1790s, Rose Hill was renamed Parramatta, based on a local Aboriginal word that meant 'place where eels lie down'. The governor's mansion was established there in 1799. All of this suggests that Parramatta was meant to turn into the Big City, with Sydney a mere coastal offshoot. That's certainly how Parramattans view the situation today.

Parramatta was declared a city in 1938, and even though the space between it and Sydney Cove is now filled with suburbs, it still operates as if it were a separate entity. The Parramatta area has a population of nearly two million and is often described as 'the engine room of Sydney'. Parramatta is the central business district for the suburbs where new families go to build houses cheaply, so its population tends to be younger than the city average. During the 1980s, Parramatta became the fastest-growing commercial centre in Australia. Many Sydney corporations have established second head-quarters there.

The western suburbs, of which Parramatta is the capital, look and feel different from the rest of Sydney. They're flat broad expanses of houses on quarter-acre blocks interspersed with shopping malls. The car is king, because the distances between work and home are greater and public transport is inadequate.

The 'westies' enjoy amusements which are barely known to other Sydney residents. They'd rather cruise along the Nepean River to the Nepean Gorge than float on Sydney Harbour. Australia's Wonderland, built at a cost of $125 million, is the mother of all amusement parks and its wildlife centre is a tourist magnet. The Penrith Panthers Club is a world unto itself, occupying 100 hectares of land, with five restaurants, two nightclubs, 13 tennis courts, a golf course, an artificial beach and three lakes (one with fishing and one with water skiing).

Parramatta itself has the greatest concentration of historic sites of any suburb. The best place for a Sunday stroll is around Parramatta Park, which contains Old Government House (1799), and then to Australia's oldest cemetery in O'Connell Street, Hambledon Cottage (1824) in Hassall Street, Experiment Farm Cottage (1830) in Ruse Street, and Elizabeth Farm (1793) in Alice Street. Then you can reward yourself with lunch at Courtney's Brasserie in Horwood Place or Barnaby's, overlooking the river in Phillip Street.

And forget about 26 January as a Sydney historic event. Parramatta celebrates Foundation Day on 2 November, the day in 1788 when Governor Phillip established Australia's first successful government farm and began to think there was hope for the colony after all.

88
the Blue Mountains

*P*enrith is the western limit of Sydney; after that the land goes rapidly upwards. Governor Macquarie tried to name the mountains the Carmarthen Hills, after a beauty spot in his native Scotland, but everybody else called them the Blue Mountains, because in summer they look that colour from Sydney (due to the effect of sunlight through gasses emitted from the mountain plants). Officially, they are part of the Great Dividing Range, and made mostly of sandstone.

By the late 19th century, the Mountains had become Sydney's holiday playground, reached in a two-hour train journey and dotted with grand hotels (such as the Carrington at Katoomba and the Hydro Majestic at Medlow Bath) from which people went bushwalking. They fell out of favour in the early 1960s, when cheap jet travel encouraged Sydneysiders to travel further for their holiday entertainment. But now the Mountains are hot again, the preferred destination for dirty weekenders and for gourmets who rationalise that the walking and the clean air justify gluttony in the interesting restaurants that have started opening there.

The Blue Mountains are called a national park, which supposedly covers 250 000 hectares, but the area actually consists of a bunch of English-looking villages strung along a railway line, surrounded by semi-wilderness. The key towns are Leura, Katoomba, Blackheath and Mount Victoria. The key restaurants are Cleopatra at Blackheath (trad French), Vulcan's at Blackheath (roasts with an Asian influence) and Darley's at Lillianfels Guesthouse in Katoomba (modernised French).

The trendy way to stay nowadays is in a guest house such as the Victoria and Albert at Mount Victoria, the Little Company at Leura, Lilianfels at Katoomba, or Cleopatra at Blackheath. Bunches of friends and big families arrange short rentals of cottages through local real estate agents. However, for the 19th century grand hotel experience there's still the Hydro Majestic at Medlow Bath, somewhat diminished by tacky renovations but anthropologically interesting.

The key tourist experiences are: the Three Sisters (near Katoomba), a rock formation which comes with a dubious Aboriginal legend about a witch-doctor father who turned his daughters to stone to stop a bunyip eating them; the Scenic Railway, a ride down a sheer cliff-face near Katoomba; Govett's Leap, a spectacular waterfall at Blackheath; the Jenolan Caves, extensive limestone caverns southwest of Mount Victoria; the gracious gardens of Mount Wilson; the home of the sexy artist Norman

Lindsay at Springwood, now a museum; and the four-hour walk from the waterfall at Wentworth Falls, once trudged by Charles Darwin.

If it's pouring, you can take in the giant screen cinema called The Edge, near Katoomba, which shows a film on the Blue Mountains wilderness, including scenes of the recently discovered Wollemi pines, which were supposed to have died out 150 million years ago. Then you can return to your roaring fire and your Devonshire tea.

89
Watsons Bay

*e*xtremity is an appropriate word for Sydney's eastern limit, because it includes the city's favourite suicide spot—a high cliff, known as The Gap, overlooking the Tasman Sea. Just near the jumping off point is the cheery sight of the anchor from the ship *Dunbar*, which was wrecked on the rocks below in 1857, with 122 people drowned and only one survivor.

The number of people either falling or jumping from the Gap became such a problem during the Depression that the NSW police formed the Cliff Rescue Unit, trained both in climbing and in persuading people that life isn't that bad. The unit turned into the Police Rescue Squad, more recently immortalised in a TV series.

The area around The Gap is called Watsons Bay, named after Robert Watson, a First Fleet sailor who was appointed Sydney's first harbourmaster. After being sacked for theft in 1815, he started a fishing village on the south headland of Port Jackson. A few of the wooden cottages from that period can still be seen in the streets near Camp Cove beach, but by the 1860s, Watsons Bay and its adjoining suburb of Vaucluse had become the retreat of Sydney's wealthy.

The key streets these days are Wentworth and Coolong Roads, where the waterfront villas regularly sell for between five and ten million dollars each. The area is best known internationally for Doyle's restaurant, which gets shown in TV documentaries because of its harbour view, but which is just an overcrowded and overpriced fish and chippery. Instead of queuing to sit at its tables, sensible people buy a takeaway box on Watson's Bay wharf and picnic in front of the same view.

There's a terrific walk from the *Dunbar* anchor through bushland to the tip of South Head, past Camp Cove and back through narrow streets to the pretty beaches at Parsley Bay and Nielsen Park.

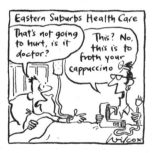

90
Barrenjoey

*a*t the northern tip of Sydney you have every chance of seeing fairy penguins, sea eagles, goannas, whistling kites and Aboriginal rock paintings. You'll also get a fabulous surf and an interesting lunch. It's worth devoting a day to Barrenjoey, Palm Beach and Ku-ring-gai National Park.

Go early and start the day at the top—Barrenjoey (which means a young kangaroo according to Arthur Phillip's hearing of the local Aboriginal language). It was once a high rocky island but now it's connected to Palm Beach by a peninsula of sand. A customs post was established on it in 1843 to stop smuggling in and out of Pittwater and a lighthouse was built there in 1881 as shipping between the Hawkesbury River and Sydney Harbour got busier. Now one of Sydney's most invigorating walks involves climbing the rocky path up to the sandstone lighthouse where one of Sydney's most inspiring views—of Broken Bay, Pittwater and Palm Beach—is waiting at the top.

In the 19th century, the Palm Beach area was a vegetable plantation and it got few visitors until the cart track was turned into a road in the 1920s. Then it became the fashionable retreat for swimmers willing to travel a long way for privacy. Now it's lined with the weekenders of millionaires, who do their social drinking at the exclusive Cabbage Tree Club on the beachfront. Not far from the club is the excellent Beach Road restaurant, which lets you eat on a verandah and imagine you're a local.

After lunch you ought to catch the little ferry from Palm Beach wharf on the Pittwater side of the Peninsula to float past escapist settlements such as Mackerel Beach and Coasters Beach. Get off at The Basin—it's the entry to Ku-ring-gai National Park. The Basin Trail leads briskly to Sydney's best preserved rock art. Catch the ferry back to Palm Beach a couple of hours later, and then the Route 190 bus for a 90-minute ride back to town.

91
the Royal National Park

*t*he southern boundary of Sydney is marked by what is technically the oldest national park in the world. The Royal was officially dedicated in 1879, ahead of the official dedication of Yellowstone National Park in the US, but we'd be dishonest if we didn't admit that Yellowstone had been functioning as a national park since 1872.

In any case, the modern notion of a national park as a place of untouched wilderness didn't apply for most of the Royal's history. Logging was carried out well into the early 20th century. There are still early 20th century cottages scattered along its coastline, built by escapists or fishing addicts. And there are still deer roaming around amongst the native wildlife, the result of an early program to make the colony more like 'home'. The English-looking village of Audley was built in the middle of the park, with an Edwardian pavilion from 1901 and a dance hall from 1920, which now serves as an information centre and a place to buy food and rent canoes. The Royal seems able to survive anything. In 1994, more than two-thirds of it was burnt out in disastrous bushfires, but within three years it had almost completely regenerated.

The park covers 15 000 hectares. You can drive into it, but the more interesting approach involves taking the train to Cronulla (a lovely, if overdeveloped, beach whose name means 'place of pink shells') and then catching a little ferry across to the village of Bundeena. You can follow Scarborough Street to the track into the park and, if you're energetic, do a 13 km walk along Marley Beach and Garie Beach to Garrawarra. At Jibbon Head, just east of Bundeena, there are rock carvings of kangaroos and other animals done by the Tharawal people 5000 years ago. The Tharawal, and the kangaroos, have disappeared from the area. The lyrebirds and the wildflowers remain.

92
underground

*f*or those who enjoy seeing how the great and the glorious ended up, Sydney offers a wealth of graveyards. Let me recommend four . . .

Australia's oldest cemetery is in the grounds of the now vanished St John's Church in O'Connell Street, Parramatta. The earliest still identifiable grave belongs to Henry Dodd, butler to Governor Arthur Phillip, who died in 1791. There's a variety of convicts and early settlers, including D'Arcy Wentworth (a doctor on the First Fleet and father of the political crusader William Charles Wentworth) and Samuel Marsden (known as 'the flogging parson', who joined John Macarthur in founding Australia's wool industry).

The cemetery at Gore Hill (on the Pacific Highway, near the Royal North Shore Hospital) is known as 'a headstone history book'. The first known burial there was in 1877, and it contains Louisa King, Sydney's first female pharmacist, and John Sulman, an important architect of the late 19th century.

The most spectacular cemetery is Waverley, established in 1877 on the cliffs between Bronte and Clovelly beaches. It contains the graves of the

republican author Henry Lawson, the poet Dorothea Mackellar (who wrote 'I Love a Sunburnt
country'), and the aeronautical pioneer Lawrence
Hargrave. There's also an elaborate memorial to the
convicts transported from Ireland after the rebellion
of 1798. And a gravestone carved in the shape of a
person about to dive into a pool honours the first
woman to win an Olympic gold medal for
Australia, Fanny Durack (who did the Australian
crawl at the 1912 Olympics).

Sydney's biggest cemetery is Rookwood, sprawling over about 315 hectares near Lidcombe railway
station. Founded in 1867, it now contains a million
resting Sydneysiders, divided into sections according
to religion and nationality. Until 1948, special
funeral trains used to run there from a mortuary
station, which still can be seen near Central
Railway. It's worth making a Sunday picnic there
to seek out Sydney politicians, entertainers and
tycoons, and to read blunt epitaphs such as
'STREWTH', and 'BE READY MATES', and the
one for a spelling reformer named Jacob Pitman
(brother of the inventor of shorthand), who died in
1890: 'Ferst minister in theez Koloniz ov the Dok-
trinz ov the Sekond or Niu Kristian Church'. Earlier
this century, it was common for Sydneysiders com-
plaining of illness to say they were 'as crook as
Rookwood'.

93
weather

S ydney doesn't go in for climatic extremes but it
is famous for sweltering late summer humidity,
which, at an average of 69 per cent, is second only
to that of tropical Darwin. Often enough Sydneysiders are saved by the arrival of the summer wind
we call the Southerly Buster, which roars through
in the late afternoon with spattering rains and can
bring temperatures down by as much as five degrees
centigrade in an hour. On average, however, the
wind speed in summer is 12.3 km per hour, which
puts Sydney way behind Perth in puff.

It is the second wettest capital city after Darwin
if you measure by amount of rain (1223 mm a year)
but only the third wettest after Hobart and Melbourne if you measure by the number of rainy days
(138 a year). Sydney rain tends to come in intense
bursts, sometimes lasting days, rather than the
regular drizzle they get in the southern capitals.

Sydney averages 7.2 hours of sunshine a day in
summer and 6.3 in winter, which also makes it
sunnier than Melbourne and Hobart.

Temperatures range from a low of 8 degrees centigrade in mid winter (July) to a high of 26 in mid
summer (January). The record for the highest

temperature was 45.3 on 15 January 1931, and the record low was −4.4 on 4 July 1893.

The wettest 24 hours on record was on 5 August 1986 when 327 mm or more than 13 inches of rain fell (six people were killed and 1500 people were evacuated from their homes in floods).

Sydney's wettest month is March, while the driest month, with the lowest humidity and temperatures comfortably around 16 degrees, is September. That's when the year 2000 Olympics will be held.

94
time

*n*o wonder we like to say Sydney is ahead of the rest of the world. When we're getting up in the morning, Londoners are just going to bed on the night before, and Los Angeleans haven't even started yesterday's lunch. Only New Zealanders lead their lives ahead of us—you have to add two hours to Sydney time to calculate the time in Auckland. Subtract half an hour to get the time in Adelaide, subtract two hours for Perth, one hour for Tokyo, two hours for Hong Kong, ten hours for London, 15 hours for New York, and 18 hours for LA.

All that is a simplification, of course. On the last Sunday in October, Sydney clocks go back one hour with the introduction of daylight saving time, and stay that way until the last Sunday in March. Which makes Brisbane one hour ahead of us, because Queensland is the only Australian state that does not have daylight saving. It also makes London only eight hours behind us during our summer. But then during our winter, northern countries introduce their own forms of daylight saving, which means, for example, that London is ten hours behind us between June and October.

95
getting around

S ydney uses public transport more than any other
Australian city—23 per cent of us ride a bus,
train or ferry every weekday, spending an average of
one hour and four minutes a day getting between
home and work and back. That's because, however
much we may grumble about it, Sydney's public
transport system has finally become efficient, after
years of tinkering with a variety of vehicles. The
various modes of transport have got their act together
enough to operate a single phone number (131 500)
which answers all questions on timetables and
connections.

These are the different elements of the system:

☆ **TRAINS.** The first
government-owned
railway in the British
Empire opened in 1855
between Redfern and
Parramatta, and from
then on the lines kept
snaking through the

They say trains may be less frequent, but more regular.

So it should be along any day now

BLAC

LACKTOWN

Wilcox

suburbs, with the north shore line opening in
1890—although the eastern suburbs line was
not completed until 1979. By the year 2000

you'll be able to catch a train to Sydney airport. The first electric service started in 1926. Now, Sydney's trains carry 800 000 passengers a day between 4am and midnight on 2000 services over 1700 km of track. The best city stations from which to start a suburban journey are either Town Hall in midtown, or Central at the southern end of the CBD (also the place for trains out of Sydney). The prettiest train journeys are from Town Hall to Waitara on the north shore line, and from Central to Wollongong on the south coast line.

☆ **TRAMS.** The first trams, drawn by horses, were introduced to Sydney in 1861. They were replaced in 1879 by steam-powered models and then, after 1890, by electric models that drew their power from wires strung above the street. The speed was too much for some people. A commentator in the early 1890s, the Hon Harold Finch-Hatton, wrote: 'The trams rush down the most crowded thoroughfares, terrifying horses and killing on an average about two passengers a week, besides maiming numerous other ones'. Nevertheless, tram rides were favourite Sydney experiences for the first half of the 20th century, inspiring a local synonym for speedy departure, 'shooting through like a Bondi tram'. But in the 1950s, the state government, in the grip of a misguided notion of progress, decided to replace them with buses, and the last tram ran on 26 February 1961 from La Perouse to the Randwick workshops. Now, the rattlers are back, in a sleeker form called 'light rail'. In mid 1997, a service started between Central railway station and the Sydney Fish Markets, via Haymarket, Darling Harbour and the casino, and there are plans to extend the line as far as Lilyfield in the inner western suburbs. One day Sydneysiders are sure to talk about 'shooting through like a Lilyfield light rail'.

☆ **BUSES.** The 1500 buses in the Sydney fleet cover the gaps where the trains don't reach. Buses to the eastern and western suburbs mostly leave from Circular Quay, while buses going north leave from near Wynyard railway station. There are two special tourist services: the red Sydney Explorer, which shuttles around the main inner-city sights, and the blue Bondi and Bay Explorer around the eastern beaches. Sydney's prettiest (and longest) bus ride is Route 190 from Wynyard to Palm Beach along the northern beaches.

☆ **FERRIES.** The first ferry service was a sailing boat that started shuttling between Sydney Cove and Parramatta in 1793, replaced by a steam launch in 1831. The Manly ferry, in the form of a steam-powered paddle-wheeler, started operations in 1847. Nowadays, some 30 government-run craft traverse Sydney

Harbour and the adjoining rivers, starting from
Circular Quay and reaching Parramatta,
Balmain, Darling Harbour, Neutral Bay,
Mosman, Manly and Watsons Bay.

In addition to these mainstream services, there
are taxis (which you can hail on the street or order
by phone and which are hardest to find around 3pm
when the drivers change shifts); water taxis (very
expensive and best shared by a group); and the
monorail (which runs in a tiny loop round Darling
Harbour and the mid city, and which is more of a
toytown ride than a useful service).

Or you could use a car. It's not much use in the
inner city, where parking is hard to find and fines
are high. The speed limit in built-up areas is 60 km
per hour and on country highways is 110 kmh. For
getting out of town, the main arteries are: northwards on the Pacific Highway for Gosford, Newcastle and Brisbane; westwards on Parramatta
Road, which turns into the Great Western Highway
for the Blue Mountains; southwards on King Street,
Newtown, which turns into the Princes Highway to
Wollongong and Melbourne; south westwards on
Canterbury Road, which turns into the Hume
Highway to Canberra; and southwards on South
Dowling Street, which turns into the freeway to the
airport.

96
communications

*a*ustralia's first post office was established on 28 April 1809 in the Sydney home of Isaac Nichols, assistant to the Naval Officer. He held all the mail that arrived from overseas and charged one shilling for each letter when it was collected. Sydney got its first postman, who delivered the mail twice a week in a horse and cart, in 1828. By then, there were post offices as far afield as Parramatta, Windsor and Penrith. They started selling postage stamps in 1850.

For most of the 20th century, Sydney people got two mail deliveries every weekday and one on Saturday, but in 1968, deliveries dropped to once a day and, in 1974, the Saturday deliveries stopped. Now, suburban post offices have expanded themselves into souvenir shops to make up for the revenue lost when we started using fax machines and private courier services.

These days a stamp for an ordinary letter costs 45 cents, and Australia Post claims that a letter posted in

Sydney before 6pm should reach another Sydney suburb the next day, and the rest of Australia in two days. Mail to the USA or Europe takes about seven days.

The first alternative to communicating by post appeared in 1858, with the opening of a telegraph line between the Sydney GPO and South Head. Telegraph lines spread across the country, and then around the world. But their doom was signalled in January 1878 when the NSW Superintendent of Telegraphs successfully tested a newfangled device called a telephone line between Sydney and Kurnell. The first phone exchange opened in November 1880, and the first public phone box opened at the Sydney GPO in 1893.

Nowadays, it costs about 25 cents to call from home, about 40 cents to make a local call from a public phone, and a lot more to use a mobile phone—which hasn't stopped Sydneysiders from becoming addicted to them. To save carrying change, you can buy phone cards from newsagents. The main phone company is Telstra, two-thirds owned by the federal government. Its major private competitor is Optus. The information number is 013.

97
events

*W*hile the precise dates of many Sydney activities vary from year to year, here's a rough calendar of how life unfolds in the Harbour city.

JANUARY
☆ New Years Day public holiday on or near 1 January.

☆ The Sydney Festival, with stage shows, talks, displays and cabaret, runs all month at venues around the harbour.

☆ The NSW Open Tennis at White City Courts, Paddington.

☆ Opera in the Park, held in the Domain on a Saturday evening.

☆ Symphony under the Stars in the Domain on a Saturday evening.

☆ Australia Day public holiday on 26 January (commemorating Arthur Phillip raising the flag in Port Jackson).

FEBRUARY
☆ The school year begins.

☆ The Sydney Gay & Lesbian Mardi Gras cultural festival goes all month, culminating in the parade along Oxford Street on a Saturday night.

☆ Chinese New Year.

MARCH

☆ Clean Up Australia day, where people are asked to devote a Sunday to picking up rubbish, particularly from the Harbour.

☆ International Woman's Day march.

☆ Saint Patrick's Day parade, with festivities concentrated around the Rocks.

☆ Royal Easter Show, now held at Homebush, where rural people show off their farming triumphs to city people.

☆ Public holidays for Good Friday and Easter Monday

☆ School holidays start.

☆ Daylight Saving ends—clocks go back an hour on the last Sunday of March.

APRIL

☆ April Fools Day.

☆ Walk Against Want, held on a Sunday, raises funds for Community Aid Abroad.

☆ Second school term begins.

☆ National Trust's Heritage Week, with historical displays.

☆ Anzac Day public holiday (25 April) with a march and services to remember Australians who died in wars.

MAY

☆ Sydney Writers' Festival, in which local and

visiting authors discuss their work, held in venues around the Rocks.

☆ Islamic New Year.

☆ Mothers' Day on the second Sunday.

JUNE

☆ Sydney Film Festival, two weeks of non-stop viewing in the State Theatre.

☆ World Environment Day and Wilderness Society badge day.

☆ Queen's birthday public holiday.

☆ Winter school holidays begin.

JULY

☆ National Aboriginal and Islander Week, culminating in Aboriginal Day around 11 July.

☆ International Piano Competition, organised by the Conservatorium of Music.

☆ The Biennale, a celebration of art, held in even-numbered years.

☆ Third school term starts.

AUGUST

☆ Red Nose Day fundraising for Sudden Infant Death Syndrome.

☆ City to Surf Fun Run, with thousands of people in a Sunday marathon from the Sydney Town Hall to Bondi.

SEPTEMBER

☆ Spring starts.

☆ Fathers Day on the first Sunday.

☆ Education Week, when parents can visit schools.

☆ School holidays start.
☆ Cultural Olympiad arts festival.
☆ Festival of the Winds—kite flying at Bondi.
☆ Rugby league grand final.
☆ Sleaze Ball, a big party offering a gay time for all and fund-raising for Mardi Gras.

OCTOBER

☆ Jewish New Year.
☆ Labor Day public holiday (around 6 October).
☆ Fourth school term starts.
☆ Higher School Certificate public exams start.
☆ Daylight Saving starts—clocks go forward an hour on the last Sunday of October.

NOVEMBER

☆ Melbourne Cup, the day when Sydney stops to bet on a Victorian horse race.
☆ Parramatta Foundation Festival.

DECEMBER

☆ School year ends, summer holidays start.
☆ Carols by Candlelight on a Saturday night in the Domain.
☆ Christmas Day and Boxing Day public holidays.
☆ Sydney to Hobart yacht race sets off from Sydney Harbour on 26 December with 200 starters.

98
the Olympics

*t*he first Australian to win a gold medal in the modern Olympics (because an Australian could hardly have won anything in the ancient Olympics) was Frederick Lane, who swam to glory in the 200 metres freestyle and the 200 metres obstacle race in the Paris Olympics of 1900. He'd taken up swimming after being saved from drowning in Sydney Harbour at the age of four. Lane was also the first man to swim 100 yards in one minute.

We expect many more such feats to occur between Friday 21 September and Sunday 1 October 2000 when Sydney will host the next Olympics. There will be 28 sports played by 10 200 athletes from 200 countries. They'll be in two main areas: a site at Homebush in the western suburbs for 15 sports (including athletics, swimming and tennis) and assorted sites in the inner city, particularly around Darling Harbour, for ten sports including basketball, boxing and weightlifting. The sailing will be held off Rushcutters Bay in the inner east, and the cycling will be between Sydney Football Stadium and Bronte Beach.

The 660-hectare Homebush site, which will include the 110 000-seat main stadium, used to be a racecourse, a brickworks, an armaments depot and an abattoir. There are daily bus tours, leaving from Strathfield railway station, for anyone who'd like to check out building progress (phone 9735 4344).

The cost of staging the Sydney Olympics will be about $5.2 billion, of which taxpayers will pay one-third and the rest will be raised through business sponsorships and ticket sales. The average ticket price will be about $60 (ranging from $10 for bad seats at boring events to $500 for the glamour events). A total of six and half million tickets will be sold. Sponsors, organisers and athletes will get first claim on them.

At this point, the events to which ordinary Sydneysiders are likely to gain access are baseball, boxing, soccer, sailing, canoeing, horseriding and rowing. Don't even think about the swimming, the gymnastics or the opening ceremony. And bear in mind that even if you do get a ticket, you won't be able to drive to the Games. The only access will be by train, bus or ferry. And allow an extra hour to get through the security checks.

99
Olympericks

a t the end of the Olympic Games in Atlanta in 1996, Australia's contribution to the closing ceremony included a group of schoolchildren riding bicycles with giant, colourful, rubber kangaroos on the back. Some Sydney people found this amusing, some were embarrassed that we might have looked kitschy in the eyes of the world. Ric Birch, the designer for the 2000 festivities, promised to maintain the tone of 'likeable larrikinism'. This provoked concern that the opening ceremony for the year 2000 Games should be designed with good taste as well as patriotic sensibility. The 'Stay in Touch' column in *The Sydney Morning Herald* ran a contest asking readers to describe the 2000 opening ceremony in a limerick. By way of inspiration, the column invented these:

A Hoist hung with red rubber roos
Revolves in primordial ooze.
And instead of a song,
We'll all clap our thongs,
Then get stuck into free tins of booze.
As the world packs its bags for Australia,
We must hurry and build, inter alia,
A Big Kylie and Mel,
Nicole, Ray and Elle,

Each one nude but for Veg-covered genitalia.

And these were among the winning entries:

'Australia regrets,' said the fax,
'That although we have tried to the max,
The Games can't go on.
It was all a big con.
Howard's funding cuts gave them the axe.'
from Susan Anthony of Waterloo
There were roos and emus playing yo-yos,
Wombats and galahs wearing Speedos,
But the biggest surprise,
Seen with my own eyes,
Was a corroboree danced by Iced Vo-Vos.
from Lex Watson of East Balmain
To open the Games get Diana
'Cause her name rhymes quite well with goanna
And to wind up the thing
She'd sing 'God Save The King'
Played by Charlie and Cam on piana.
from Tony Thurbron of North Nowra
Round the track, the gun lobby in caps
Shoot at rows full of package tour Japs,
While in the arena,
Priests play with boys' wieners
And pray that their memories lapse.
from Tom Simpson of Bondi
Blue singleted blokes trooping slow,
Jack hammers and shovels in tow,
With Olympian gravity
Dig a dirty great cavity
Half fill it with concrete, then go.
from Les Ross of Naremburn

100
the future

So it's Monday, October the second, in the year 2000. We've woken up, swept up, treated our hangovers from the Olympic closing parties of the night before, and now we're wondering: what are we doing for the rest of the 21st century? If all the promises made by the politicians and the planners during the 1990s were true, we should be living in a city that's close to perfect.

There'll be no traffic problems in midtown because an Eastern Distributor will be running underneath the city. At the rundown Central railway end, the footpaths will have been widened and lined with cafes. The old piers around Circular Quay and the industrial docks at Walsh Bay will house new hotels, theatres and shops. There'll be a complex of 'marina apartments' around Woolloomooloo Bay. All the 'black holes' that were dug around the city in the 1980s will have sprouted postmodern office/shopping/living centres. And Hyde Park will have expanded eastwards,

regaining some of the spaces that were cut off by roads in the late 19th century.

Because elegant new apartment blocks will have replaced the glut of office space in the Central Business District, there'll be life around the harbour—24-hour shops and cafes will have opened to meet the needs of the new residents, making Sydney more like a European or South American city. Governor Lachlan Macquarie will look down and feel his grand plan has finally been achieved.

Sydney Harbour will be a clean waterway in which we can catch fish that won't poison us. The beaches will be totally turd-free. In 1997, the NSW Premier, Bob Carr, promised to spend $3 billion on an urban wastewater and stormwater clean-up program, including $1.6 billion to overhaul Sydney's sewerage pipes and treatment facilities and $375 million to eliminate sewerage overflows into the harbour. He said: 'I want my legacy as a premier to be the saving of the state's forests and the cleaning up of the state's waterways.'

Sydney will rival Hollywood as a film-making capital, churning out movies and TV sitcoms from the giant Fox studios at Moore Park. By 2000, Sydney's population will be four million. The major growth in new housing will be in five areas: Rouse Hill in the northwest (expected to have 40 000 new residents by 2005); Ultimo and Pyrmont in the inner city (18 000 new residents by 2005, mostly in apartment blocks); Roseberry in the inner south (15 000);

Harrington Park in the southwest (11 000); and Warriewood in the north (4000).

Trains will run to Bondi Beach, the airport and all those western suburbs that public transport never managed to reach before. Not that we'll be getting out much, since we'll be doing our shopping and socialising in cyberspace, thanks to the cables threaded over and under our streets.

The planet has just lived through what's been called 'the American century', during which New York was the capital of the world. It has been argued that the 21st looks like being 'the Australian century'. And if that's the case, no city is better prepared to become the capital of the world than Sydney.

index

INDEX

INDEX

INDEX

David Dale
**THE 100 THINGS EVERYONE NEEDS TO KNOW
ABOUT AUSTRALIA – 1998 EDITION**

The core knowledge for every Australian and the basic
briefing for every visitor.

Here's the essential stuff you learned at school and then
forgot, plus all the useful stuff they never taught you:

Our biggest, wettest, smartest, richest and most
mysterious places, people and achievements;

How Australia changed from being one of the dullest
countries on earth to one of the liveliest, in a single
generation;

The taxes we pay and how our governments spend them;

The truth about our icons: Vegemite, Ned Kelly, meat
pies, the Hills Hoist and Elle Macpherson;

Why the tall poppy syndrome is our healthiest national
trait;

The only two politicians and the only two billionaires
that matter;

How Australians talk, eat, gamble and drink.

AVAILABLE FROM PAN MACMILLAN

David Dale
ESSENTIAL PLACES

The Hindus use the word darshana *for the mysterious ecstasy generated in the presence of a holy place. Modern western travellers may experience darshana under more secular conditions. The first time I felt it was in the flat of Sigmund Freud, in Vienna, when I realised that this room produced the most influential theory of the 20th century – that human behaviour is largely driven by the unconscious mind . . . I decided that from then on, I would travel in search of darshana.*

Essential Places is a collection of journeys through a landscape of ideas – half travel book, half guide to the icons of our age.

From Kowloon to California, from Charles Darwin's garden to Vincent Van Gogh's asylum, from the birthplace of the skyscraper to the tomb of Tutankhamun, David Dale seeks out the places every serious traveller must try to reach in order to understand the modern world. He brings together Archimedes and Marilyn Monroe, politics and pasta, fung shui and future shock in twenty-six voyages of the mind and body.

AVAILABLE FROM PAN MACMILLAN

Lisa Clifford and Mandy Webb
WALKING SYDNEY

THE COMPLETE, COMPREHENSIVE AND UP-TO-
DATE GUIDE TO SYDNEY'S MOST BEAUTIFUL,
COLOURFUL AND FASCINATING WALKS

Sydney is a city meant for walking. From gentle strolls in
the Botanic Gardens to day-long hikes through unspoilt
National Park bushland, Sydney offers a whole range of
incomparable walks. *Walking Sydney* details 25 of the
city's best walks, covering everything from dramatic
clifftop paths and golden beaches, historic sights and
Aboriginal rock carvings to internationally renowned
museums, galleries and shops.

Each walk has its own easy-to-follow map, along with
key facts on the walk itself, including approximate
walking times, facilities along the way, how to get to and
from the walk's start point, wheelchair access and what
to expect in the way of terrain. There are also detailed
descriptions of points of interest along the way, and
information on the history and background of many of
Sydney's most fascinating sights. Catering for walkers of
all ages and all interests, *Walking Sydney* is a must for
visitors and Sydneysiders alike.

AVAILABLE FROM PAN MACMILLAN